THE
GLUTEN-FREE
NUTRITION GUIDE

TRICIA THOMPSON, M.S., RD

New York   Chicago   San Francisco   Lisbon   London   Madrid   Mexico City
Milan   New Delhi   San Juan   Seoul   Singapore   Sydney   Toronto

The **McGraw·Hill** Companies

Library of Congress Cataloging-in-Publication Data

Thompson, Tricia.
　The gluten-free nutrition guide / by Tricia Thompson.
　　　p.　　cm.
　Includes bibliograhical references.
　ISBN-13: 978-0-07-154541-9 (alk. paper)
　ISBN-10: 978-0-07-154541-7 (alk. paper)
　1. Gluten-free diet—Popular works.　　2. Gluten-free foods—Popular
works.　　I. Title.

RM237.86.T56　　2008
613.2′8—dc22　　　　　　　　　　　　　　　　2008010722

1　2　3　4　5　6　7　8　9　10　11　12　13　14　15　16　17　18　19　20　21　　FGR/FGR　0　9　8

ISBN　978-0-07-154541-9
MHID　　　0-07-154541-7

McGraw-Hill books are available at special quantity discounts to use as premiums and sales promotions or for use in corporate training programs. To contact a representative, please visit the Contact Us pages at www.mhprofessional.com.

The information contained in this book is intended to provide helpful and informative material on the subject addressed. It is not intended to serve as a replacement for professional medical advice. A health-care professional should be consulted regarding your specific situation.

This book is printed on acid-free paper.

To my husband, Dave, and son, Marcus, who are constant sources of support and inspiration.
To my father, Robert Spurr, who taught by example how life is meant to be lived.

Contents

Preface

THIS BOOK AIMS to accomplish two things: First, I hope to provide you with the information you need to eat a healthful, gluten-free diet. Second, I want to provide you with the research and evidence-based information you need to avoid common areas of confusion about the gluten-free diet. This book tells you about the best available scientific information—the same information available to physicians and dietitians. Instead of simply telling you what you should and should not eat, I present information that allows you to make your own decisions. With a little guidance and a little thought, following the gluten-free diet can be very healthful and not at all stressful.

I have been researching and writing about celiac disease and the gluten-free diet for twelve years. During this time, my work has focused on the controversial aspects of the diet, including whether oats and wheat starch should be allowed, as well as the nutritional quality of the diet. While much attention has been paid to what foods can and cannot be included in a gluten-free diet, little attention has been paid to whether the diet is nutritious. In fact, a gluten-free diet can be very healthful, but certain nutrients might be lacking. In 2005, my colleagues and I conducted a study whose results indicated that many gluten-free diets lack necessary levels of fiber, iron, calcium, and B vitamins. This book will show you how to make sure these vital nutrients make their way into your own diet.

Throughout the book, features titled "In My Opinion" will let you know my take on various topics under debate, including whether you should eat oats and wheat starch, and what alternatives are available for Communion wafers. These viewpoints are not intended to represent medical advice. It is important to understand that different people looking at the same information may arrive at different conclusions. For example, at the present time, opinions differ on whether oats and wheat starch should be included in a gluten-free diet. There really is no right or wrong answer. It simply comes down to personal comfort level, just as, in politics, we all fall somewhere along the spectrum of liberal to conservative.

Another feature, titled "Science Class," appears in many chapters. These items explain in greater depth some terms and concepts related to celiac disease and the gluten-free diet.

And just for fun, sections called "Historical Nuggets" are historical anecdotes about celiac disease and the gluten-free diet. I find these fascinating and thought you might, too.

I wish you peace, happiness, and health as you embark on a healthful gluten-free lifestyle.

Acknowledgments

I OWE A tremendous debt of gratitude to Philip Ruppel, president of McGraw-Hill Professional, who took an unsolicited manuscript and passed it into the appropriate hands. Those hands belong to editor Johanna Bowman, to whom I also owe much gratitude. From the beginning, she believed in this book, and it has become so much better under her guidance. Thank you to Nancy Hall, the project editor assigned, and everyone else at McGraw-Hill, whose names I do not know, who worked on this book.

A big thank-you to all the colleagues, friends, and family who contributed recipes: Susan Algert, Veronica Alicea, Pam Cureton, Melinda Dennis, Elizabeth Di Biase, Mark Dinga, Nancy Falini, Judi Kopsack, Cynthia Kupper, Anne Lee, Andrea Levario, Trisha Lyons, Natalie Mazurets, Alice Miller, Elaine Monarch, Jane Roberts, Mary Schluckebier, Mary Kay Sharrett, Betsy Spurr, and Evelyn Tribole. Their willingness to share their creativity adds personality to this book and is greatly appreciated.

A big hug to my son, Marcus, who has sat through his share of dinnertime conversations on celiac disease. As a result, he undoubtedly knows more about the nutritional quality of the gluten-free diet than any other ten-year-old (and he doesn't even have celiac disease). In fact, when a nutritionist came to his science class to speak about healthful eating and mentioned the need to eat whole grains, Marcus raised his hand and asked what whole grains a person with celiac disease could eat. Marcus already knew the answer, but he wanted to see whether the nutritionist did. She knew enough to say brown rice, but this did not satisfy Marcus, who felt she should have mentioned buckwheat and quinoa as well!

Last but not least, a huge hug to my husband, Dave, who has edited all my writings on celiac disease over the years and offered his share of tough although constructive criticism. Everyone should be so lucky to have a resident editor. My work is much better because of his efforts.

Celiac Disease and the Gluten-Free Diet: The Basics

We have learnt in the course of many years' experience in the treatment of cases of celiac disease that it makes a great difference to the patient what kind of starch-containing foodstuffs are included in the diet; in particular whether or not wheat is used.

—Willem-Karel Dicke, Dutch pediatrician and early advocate of the gluten-free diet for the treatment of celiac disease, 1953

MOST LIKELY, YOU are reading this book because you or someone you know has celiac disease. If that's the case, it may help you to know that you or your loved one is in good company. Years ago, celiac disease was considered rare in the United States. However, research conducted by Alessio Fasano at the University of Maryland Center for Celiac Research now tells us that the prevalence of celiac disease in the general U.S. population is 1 in 133. This is similar to the prevalence of celiac disease in parts of Europe. In Italy, for example, it has been reported that 1 in 250 people has celiac disease, and in Ireland the prevalence is reported to be 1 in 300.

Thanks in part to Fasano's study, celiac disease has hit the big time. In 2004, the National Institutes of Health held a consensus development conference on celiac disease, the Food and Drug Administration is currently developing a labeling rule to allow for the voluntary identification of food as gluten free, and stories about celiac disease and the gluten-free diet appear in the print media frequently. Quite frankly, there has never been a better time to be diagnosed with celiac disease.

Historical Nuggets

London physician Samuel Gee is often credited as being the first to describe celiac disease in his famous article, "On the Coeliac Affection," published in the *St. Bartholomew's Hospital Report* in 1888. However, Roman physician Aretaues may have described celiac disease as long ago as the second century, when he wrote, "If the stomach be irretentive of the food and if it pass through undigested and crude, and nothing ascends into the body, we call such persons coeliacs."

According to the American Heritage Dictionary, the word *celiac* literally means of or relating to the abdomen. *Celiac* comes from the Latin word *coeliacus*, which comes from the Greek word *koiliakos*. *Koilia* in Greek means abdomen. In the United States, the disease is spelled "celiac," while in Britain it is "coeliac."

What Is Celiac Disease?

Celiac disease, also known as celiac sprue and gluten intolerance, is a genetically based autoimmune disease characterized by sensitivity to proteins found in the cereal grains wheat, barley, and rye. Having a *genetically based* disease means that the potential to develop the disease was inherited from one or both parents. Having an *autoimmune* disease means that the body's own immune system damages tissues of the body when presented with something it views as harmful. In the case of celiac disease, the body views certain proteins found in wheat, barley, and rye as harmful.

When these grains are eaten, they trigger a response from the immune system that results in inflammation and damage to the lining of the small intestine.

Many of the nutrients found in the food we eat are absorbed in the small intestine. The lining (also called the mucosa) of the small intestine contains tiny hairlike projections called villi, which aid in the absorption of nutrients. In the case of celiac disease, these villi may become shortened, or blunted. If the villi become blunted, the body may become unable to properly absorb several nutrients, including proteins, fats, carbohydrates, vitamins, and minerals.

When the body is unable to absorb important nutrients from food (a condition called malabsorption), several conditions may arise. These may include gastrointestinal symptoms such as diarrhea, gas, bloating, and constipation. Other conditions may develop as well. For example, people with celiac disease may experience anemia (low levels of hemoglobin in the blood) caused by the body's inability to properly absorb the mineral iron or the vitamin folate, bone disease (caused by the body's inability to properly absorb the mineral calcium and/or vitamin D), and weight loss (because the body cannot properly absorb calories from the macronutrients fat, protein, and carbohydrate).

If you have been newly diagnosed with celiac disease and have never been tested for osteoporosis (a bone disease) or anemia, you may want to speak with your physician about having a bone density test and a blood workup for anemia.

Diagnosis of Celiac Disease

According to the Statement on Celiac Disease prepared by the National Institutes of Health Consensus Development Conference, a diagnosis of celiac disease requires several steps:

1. **Serologic testing.** If a physician suspects that a patient has celiac disease, the first step in the diagnostic process is often

a simple blood test. Serologic tests are useful for diagnosing celiac disease. They measure blood levels of antibodies that are found in above-normal levels in persons with celiac disease. The serologic tests that are currently considered the best are the immunoglobulin A antihuman tissue transglutaminase (IgA tTG) and the immunoglobulin A endomysial antibody immunofluorescence (IgA EMA).

2. **Intestinal biopsy.** If the results of the serologic tests are consistent with what would be found in celiac disease, the next step in the diagnostic process is an intestinal biopsy, in which tissue samples from the mucosa of the upper end (duodenum) of the small intestine are examined under a microscope for abnormalities consistent with celiac disease. Biopsy samples are collected during an upper endoscopy, an outpatient procedure performed by a gastroenterologist. The most important abnormality from the standpoint of diagnosing celiac disease is villous atrophy, or shortening of the villi that line the mucosa of the small intestine.

3. **Gluten-free diet.** If findings of the serologic tests and/or intestinal biopsy are consistent with what would be seen in celiac disease, the third step in the diagnostic process is to have the patient follow a gluten-free diet. If, together with positive serological and/or biopsy findings, the gluten-free diet reduces (and eventually resolves) any gastrointestinal symptoms the patient was experiencing, a definitive diagnosis of celiac disease can be made.

Treatment of Celiac Disease

The only available treatment for celiac disease is a gluten-free diet. This is so fundamental and important that it bears repeating with emphasis: *The only treatment for celiac disease is a gluten-free diet.*

The only controversy surrounding treatment is what exactly constitutes a gluten-free diet. (Chapter 2 covers controversial aspects of the gluten-free diet.) In the United States, a gluten-free diet is generally defined as a diet that does not include protein from wheat, barley, rye, and possibly oats.

Why It's Important to Follow a Gluten-Free Diet. When a person with celiac disease stops eating wheat, barley, and rye, the proteins that used to trigger an immune system reaction are no longer present in the body. Removing these harmful grains from the diet not only prevents further damage to the small intestinal mucosa but also allows it to heal. Intestinal villi grow back, and the body absorbs more nutrients. Any gastrointestinal symptoms that were caused by malabsorption begin to decrease, and it becomes possible to treat vitamin and mineral deficiencies that may have occurred.

Science Class

You don't need to understand cereal chemistry to follow a gluten-free diet, but you may find it helpful to understand the terms *gluten* and *prolamin*.

Gluten

From the standpoint of celiac disease, the term *gluten* is used to describe proteins found in wheat, barley, and rye that must not be eaten in a gluten-free diet. Strictly speaking, however, gluten is a protein found *only* in wheat. It is made up of groups of proteins (of two types, glutelins and prolamins), including the glutelin *glutenin* and the prolamin *gliadin*. Gluten is responsible for the "elasticity" of baked goods made with wheat flour.

The term *gluten* is sometimes used in a more general sense to describe proteins (glutelins and prolamins) found in many cereal

continued

grains. For example, you may hear or see references to corn gluten or rice gluten, both of which are fine for you to eat.

Prolamins

Prolamins are storage proteins found in many cereal grain foods. They are called storage proteins because they are a source of nutrients for developing plants. The prolamins of wheat, barley, and rye, termed *gliadin*, *hordein*, and *secalin* respectively, contain the specific amino acid sequences harmful to persons with celiac disease. However, not all prolamins are harmful. For example, the corn prolamin *zein* and the rice prolamin *orzenin* do not contain harmful amino acid sequences, so they do not trigger immune responses in persons with celiac disease.

It is important to note that while gliadin is generally implicated as the harmful fraction of gluten, glutenin also may contain amino acid sequences harmful to persons with celiac disease.

Dermatitis Herpetiformis

Dermatitis herpetiformis (DH) is a form of celiac disease involving the skin. If you have DH, you will develop extremely itchy, raised blistering skin lesions if you eat protein from wheat, barley, and rye. These lesions may occur on the outer surface of the elbows, knees, shoulders, and buttocks and are evenly distributed on both sides of the body. In most cases, the mucosa of the small intestine also is damaged, although you may not experience any gastrointestinal symptoms.

DH is diagnosed using a biopsy of the skin. If the biopsy reveals a buildup of immunoglobulin A antibodies, a diagnosis of DH can be made. Dermatitis herpetiformis is treated with a gluten-free diet as well as the medications dapsone and sulfapyridine for the skin lesions. The use of medication alone will resolve the skin but not the intestinal lesions.

What Is a Gluten-Free Diet?

Whether or not you are new to the gluten-free diet, you may feel confused by some of the conflicting information out there about what grains can and cannot be eaten on a gluten-free diet. To top things off, you may have never heard of some of the grains you are supposed to be eating, such as teff. The information provided here will help you sort out the grains you can and cannot eat and introduce you to some of the less familiar grains.

A gluten-free diet as followed in the United States does not contain protein from wheat, barley, rye, or hybrids of these grains. All other grain foods, with the possible exception of oats, are considered safe to include in a gluten-free diet. Oats are discussed in detail in Chapter 2.

GRAINS THAT CAN'T BE EATEN ON A GLUTEN-FREE DIET
* Wheat, including all types (spelt, einkorn, emmer, kamut, durum) and forms (wheat starch,* wheat bran, wheat germ, cracked wheat, crushed wheat, hydrolyzed wheat protein, farina, semolina, graham flour)
* Barley, including all forms (malt, malt syrup, malt extract)
* Rye
* Triticale (a cross between wheat and rye)

All other grains (with the possible exception of oats) can be eaten on a gluten-free diet.

---

*The Food and Drug Administration is proposing to allow wheat starch in products labeled gluten free as long as the final food product contains less than 20 parts per million of gluten. Wheat starch is discussed in detail in Chapters 2 and 3.

Historical Nugget

The gluten-free diet has not always been the treatment for celiac disease. Before the 1950s and the identification of wheat gluten as the culprit in celiac disease, the thinking was that people with celiac disease could not properly absorb carbohydrates and/or fat. A particularly interesting dietary treatment used during this time was the "banana diet," made popular by physician Sidney Haas. This diet restricted both carbohydrates (with the exception of ripe bananas) and fat. In his famous paper, "The Value of the Banana in the Treatment of Celiac Disease," published in 1924, Dr. Haas presented the following foods as a typical diet for a child with celiac disease: albumin milk, pot cheese, bananas (as many as the child would take, usually four to eight each day), oranges, vegetables, gelatin, and meat.

In his paper, Dr. Haas makes the following observation: "Of interest in connection with the present paper is the statement that in Porto Rico (sic) the town dwellers who eat much bread suffer from sprue, the farmers who live largely on bananas never." It is interesting to note that the farmers' health was credited to bananas and not to the lack of bread in their diet.

GRAINS THAT CAN BE EATEN ON A GLUTEN-FREE DIET
* ❖ Rice
* ❖ Corn
* ❖ Sorghum
* ❖ Millet
* ❖ Teff
* ❖ Wild rice

Sorghum, Millet, Teff, and Wild Rice

You are undoubtedly familiar with corn and rice but may not be so familiar with sorghum, millet, teff, and wild rice. This section briefly describes these grains, and Chapter 6 includes delicious recipes using these grains. You may have trouble finding some of these grains in your local grocery or health food store. If so, Appendix C provides some helpful links and company names, so you can order all of the grains you need.

❖ **Sorghum** has been eaten in Africa for more than four thousand years and is available as sorghum grain and sorghum flour. Sorghum flour works well in baked goods, and the whole grain may be eaten as a breakfast cereal. Sorghum may be available in your local natural-foods store. If not, you can order it from several companies listed in Appendix C, including Twin Valley Mills (twinvalleymills.com). This company is also a source of general information on sorghum and gluten-free recipes using sorghum.

❖ **Millet** has long been a staple food of Africa and India. It is available as millet flour and millet meal, both of which are light yellow. This grain tastes and looks similar to cornmeal. The flour, which has a powdery consistency, works well in baked goods. Millet may be available in your local natural-foods store. If not, it may be ordered from several companies listed in Appendix C, including Bob's Red Mill (bobsredmill.com). This company is also a source of general information on millet and gluten-free recipes using millet.

❖ **Teff** (also spelled tef) is a staple grain of Ethiopia, where it is used to make flatbread called *injera*. It is available as teff grain and teff flour. Teff flour works well in baked goods, and the grain can be cooked like rice and eaten as either a savory side dish or a sweet breakfast cereal. Teff grain is tiny and expands when cooked. This grain may be relatively difficult to find locally, but it can be ordered from suppliers in Appendix C, including The Teff Company (teffco.com). This company is also a source of general information on teff and gluten-free recipes using teff.

❖ **Wild rice** is native to North America and was used as a staple food by Native Americans. It is unrelated to rice but is often mixed with rice or may be used in place of rice in recipes. It adds nice color and chewy texture to rice dishes. This grain is generally carried by natural-foods stores and some supermarkets. It can also be ordered from companies listed in Appendix C, including Gibbs Wild Rice (gibbswildrice.com). This company also is a source of general information on wild rice and gluten-free recipes using wild rice.

Amaranth, Quinoa, and Buckwheat

Amaranth, quinoa, and buckwheat may also be eaten on a gluten-free diet. Based on plant taxonomy (a scientific plant classification system), buckwheat, amaranth, and quinoa are not true cereal grains but rather are herbs harvested for their seeds; cereal grains, by contrast, are classified as grasses. However, they are often referred to as *pseudocereals* because the fruits and seeds of these plants may be used in food (such as breads, baked goods, breakfast cereals, and pasta) in a manner similar to cooking with true cereal grains. The following list briefly describes these plants. For delicious recipes using them, see Chapter 6.

❖ **Amaranth** is available as amaranth seed, amaranth flour, amaranth bran flour, and puffed amaranth. Amaranth flour works well in baked goods, and the seed is particularly good in soups. Amaranth seed is quite small (although not as small as teff) and does not expand much when cooked. Amaranth is generally carried by natural-foods stores. It also may be ordered from sources listed in Appendix C, including Nu-World Amaranth (nuworldamaranth.com). This company also is a good source of general information on amaranth and gluten-free recipes using amaranth.

❖ **Quinoa** is available as quinoa seed, quinoa flakes, and quinoa flour. Quinoa seed is very easy to cook and is a good replacement for rice. Quinoa is generally carried by natural-foods stores and some supermarkets. It also may be ordered from sources listed in Appendix C, including the Quinoa Corporation (quinoa.net). This company also is a good source of general information on quinoa and gluten-free recipes using quinoa.

✤ **Buckwheat** is available as buckwheat flour, buckwheat flakes, buckwheat kernels, kasha (roasted dehulled buckwheat), and buckwheat groats (raw, dehulled buckwheat). Buckwheat flour works well in a variety of baked goods, and kasha works well as a side dish and mixed with other grains. Buckwheat is generally available in natural-foods stores and some supermarkets. It also may be ordered from sources listed in Appendix C, including The Birkett Mills (thebirkettmills.com). This company also is a source of general information on buckwheat and gluten-free recipes.

2

Controversial Aspects of the Gluten-Free Diet

Unfortunately there is little agreement as to what a celiac diet is. In Switzerland it is one thing, in Holland another. In this country [United States] it depends upon whom one follows—the advocates of the banana, the advocates of fat restriction, or those who stress restriction of certain forms of carbohydrate.

—L. Emmett Holt, M.D., American pediatrician, 1955

THERE IS NO universally agreed upon gluten-free diet. Worldwide, there is scientific debate about what constitutes a gluten-free diet, particularly whether wheat starch and oats should be allowed.

The information in this chapter should give you a clearer picture of how wheat starch and oats fit into the gluten-free spectrum and should help you decide whether you want to include them in your diet.

All About Wheat Starch

Worldwide, wheat starch is one of the most controversial foods in the gluten-free diet. If you live in the United States, you may be confused about why the Food and Drug Administration is considering allowing wheat starch in foods labeled gluten free.

A large part of the controversy over wheat starch concerns the threshold level of tolerance for gluten—what amount of gluten may be consumed daily over time without damaging the mucosa of the small intestine. Unfortunately, at this time, there really is no clear answer, as research is lacking in this area.

In some countries, including those in the United Kingdom and Scandinavia, specially manufactured gluten-free foods may contain what is often referred to as "Codex wheat starch." This wheat starch has been specially processed to remove all but trace amounts of protein. Codex wheat starch is an example of a food that naturally contains gluten but has been rendered "gluten free" or "gluten-reduced" through processing and complies with the Codex Standard for Foods for Special Dietary Use for Persons Intolerant to Gluten, an international standard described later in this chapter. While Codex wheat starch still contains very small amounts of gliadin (the harmful prolamin protein of wheat), it is viewed as safe by celiac disease experts in the countries that allow its use.

Historical Nugget

In some parts of the world, wheat starch has always been allowed in a gluten-free diet, but it has never been used in products manufactured and marketed as gluten free in the United States. Instead, U.S. gluten-free products are based on grains that are naturally gluten free. One food company in particular may have been responsible for this. In 1978, Ener-G Foods (originally a manufacturer of low-protein foods for people with kidney disease) brought one of the first—if not the first—gluten-free breads to market after being approached by Elaine Hartsook, dietitian and founder of the Gluten Intolerance Group. According to the Ener-G Foods website, Hartsook asked the company to make gluten-free bread for her patients with celiac disease but was adamant that it not contain any wheat starch. Ener-G Foods complied and thereby helped set the standard for gluten-free foods in the United States.

At present, in the United States, foods containing wheat starch are not recommended for people with celiac disease, and U.S. manufacturers of gluten-free foods do not use wheat starch in their products. However, this may be changing. Under the Food and Drug Administration's (FDA's) proposed rule on use of the term *gluten free* for labeling purposes, food labeled gluten free would be allowed to contain wheat starch as long as the gluten content of the final food product was less than 20 parts per million. Chapter 3 contains a complete discussion of "gluten-free" labeling, including the FDA's proposed rule.

Wheat Starch and the Gluten-Free Diet

To understand the "wheat starch controversy," it is important to be familiar with the history of wheat starch and the gluten-free diet.

Beginning in the late 1930s, a Dutch pediatrician named Willem-Karel Dicke observed that his patients with celiac disease improved when they did not eat products containing wheat. In the late 1940s, he and his colleagues conducted feeding experiments designed to find out if wheat was the specific starch that caused problems for people with celiac disease. Patients participating in these feeding experiments were placed on diets that were similar except for the type of starch. Every few weeks, the specific starches provided to each patient were changed. Starches that caused a decrease in fat absorption and consequent increase in fat excretion were considered harmful to people with celiac disease. Based on these feeding experiments, Dicke and his colleagues found that while wheat flour had a harmful effect on their patients, wheat starch did not. Over time, however, concerns developed about the gluten content of wheat-starch-based "gluten-free" foods. Laboratory tests capable of detecting gluten confirmed that wheat-starch-based "gluten-free" foods contained small amounts of gluten.

In 2004 Finnish gastroenterologist Pekka Collin and colleagues tested twenty-six wheat-starch-based "gluten-free" flours and baked goods for gluten. Of these, only thirteen contained less than 20 parts per million of gluten (or 2 milligrams per 100 grams of product). Nine products contained between 20 parts per million and 100 parts per million of gluten, and two products contained between 100 parts per million and 200 parts per million. (For an explanation of the term *parts per million*, see "Science Class.") Whether or not these small amounts of gluten are harmful is at the heart of the wheat starch controversy.

Science Class

In simple terms, *parts per million* (abbreviated *ppm*) tells you how many parts out of a million are made up of the contaminant or ingredient in question. For example, suppose, for some reason, you want a million blue marbles. If you have a bag that contains a million marbles, and out of these million marbles, twenty are red and the rest blue, you could say your bag is "contaminated" with 20 parts per million of red marbles.

To use an example related to gluten-free eating, white bread has been reported to contain 124,000 parts per million of gluten. Assuming this amount is accurate, you can use this proportion to calculate that a one-ounce slice of white bread would contain 3,515 milligrams of gluten. Different varieties of wheat-starch-based "gluten-free" or "gluten-reduced" bread might contain 20 or 100 parts per million of gluten. One-ounce slices from each of these loaves would contain 0.6 milligram and 2.8 milligrams of gluten, respectively.

Codex Standard for Foods for Special Dietary Use for Persons Intolerant to Gluten

The Codex Standard for Foods for Special Dietary Use for Persons Intolerant to Gluten is one of the many standards established by the Codex Alimentarius Commission, a jointly run program of the Food and Agriculture Organization of the United Nations and the World Health Organization. The purpose of the commission is to develop universally accepted food standards, so that food producers around the world are meeting similar standards.

Codex standards are not legally binding in and of themselves. However, countries may choose to adopt them as their national standard. In the United States, the FDA's proposed rule for use of the term *gluten free* on food labels—that products labeled gluten free must contain less than 20 parts per million of gluten—is currently slightly stricter than the definition of gluten-free food contained in the Draft Revised Codex Standard for Foods for Special Dietary Use for Persons Intolerant to Gluten.

This Codex standard is still in draft form but is scheduled to be finalized in the summer of 2008. At the time this book went to press, the Draft Standard separates foods for special dietary use for persons intolerant to gluten into two categories: (1) gluten-free foods and (2) foods specially processed to reduce gluten content to a level above 20 up to 100 milligrams per kilogram. It is important to understand that Codex standards are not a labeling system per se. However, foods that are labeled gluten free or that have been processed to reduce gluten in countries that have adopted Codex standards as their national standard must comply with the following definitions:

❖ **Gluten-free foods:** Specially manufactured foods that are made either from naturally gluten-free ingredients only—meaning foods made from rice, corn, etc., that naturally do not contain any gluten *or* from ingredients that naturally contain gluten, such as products made from wheat, barley, rye, or crossbred varieties of these grains but are rendered (or made) gluten free during processing. Gluten-free foods may contain no more than 20 milligrams per kilogram gluten (20 parts per million).

❖ **Foods specially processed to reduce gluten content to a level above 20 up to 100 milligrams per kilogram:** Foods that are made from wheat, barley, rye, and crossbred varieties of these grains that have been specially processed to reduce gluten to a level above 20 up to 100 milligrams per kilogram (20 to 100 ppm of gluten).

In My Opinion

In my opinion, people with celiac disease should avoid wheat starch and products containing wheat starch that have been specially processed to reduce gluten to a level above 20 up to 100 milligrams per kilogram. However, if a manufacturer of wheat starch or products containing wheat starch demonstrates through testing that its products contain less than 20 parts per million of gluten (as currently proposed by the FDA), then in theory I support their consumption by people with celiac disease.

However, as a nutrition scientist, I believe it is important to point out that wheat starch is not a nutritious food product; it contains little or no fiber, vitamins, or minerals. There are so many healthful alternatives to wheat starch that I really see no need to start using it in gluten-free products. A gluten-free diet is likely to be more healthful without—rather than with—foods containing wheat starch.

Can I Eat Oats?

Another area of worldwide controversy over what constitutes a gluten-free diet is the use of oats. If you were diagnosed with celiac disease several years ago, you were probably told not to eat oats. If you were diagnosed more recently, you might have been told that certain brands of oats are OK for you to eat. So are they OK or not? The information provided in this section will help you answer that question for yourself.

Whether people with celiac disease can safely eat oats is not easily answered. Historically, oats have not been included in gluten-free diets in the United States. However, recommendations on oat consumption are changing as a result of well-designed studies conducted since 1995 that indicate that most people with celiac disease can safely eat moderate amounts of oats uncontaminated with wheat, barley, or rye. In the United States, many physicians and dietitians are advising patients that moderate amounts of certain oat products can be included in their diet. In addition, the FDA is proposing to allow oats and food containing oats to carry a "gluten-free" label as long as the final food product contains less than 20 parts per million of gluten.

Background Information on Oats and the Gluten-Free Diet

To understand the controversy about oats, you need to be familiar with the history of oats and the gluten-free diet. Dicke's classic feeding studies were the basis for the gluten-free diet as we know it today. The studies suggested that wheat flour, rye flour, and oats are harmful (barley was later added to this list). Corn flour, cornstarch, rice flour, peeled boiled potatoes, and wheat starch were determined to be harmless.

Historical Nugget

Information contained in their scientific publications suggests that Dicke and colleagues concluded that oats are harmful to patients with celiac disease based on the response to oats of *one* patient. Today, researchers require an abundance of evidence in order to draw a definitive conclusion as to the safety of a product. In recent times, numerous persons with celiac disease have been studied to try to determine the safety of oats. And we still don't have a definitive conclusion.

However, almost as soon as the gluten-free diet became the treatment for celiac disease, some physicians and researchers questioned whether oats should be included on the list of grains to avoid. Early studies that further assessed the safety of oats had findings that were contradictory—some concluding that oats are safe, others that they are harmful. However, many of these studies were not of the quality we expect from scientific studies conducted today. Most of them had to rely on now-outdated assessment procedures to determine safety.

Recent Research on the Safety of Oats

Since 1995, several studies investigating the safety of oats have used the intestinal biopsy as their method of investigation. The intestinal biopsy is considered the gold standard or best available test for diagnosing celiac disease. Participants in these studies were either newly diagnosed with celiac disease or in remission. In general, they underwent an intestinal biopsy before the start of the study and then consumed daily amounts of oats for the length of the study period. At the end of the study period, they underwent another biopsy. Biopsies from before and after the study period were compared to determine whether oat consumption had either affected recovery of the intestinal mucosa (among newly diagnosed persons with celiac disease) or adversely affected the intestinal mucosa of persons with celiac disease in remission. For the most part, these recent studies have concluded that moderate amounts of uncontaminated oats are safe for consumption by most people with celiac disease.

Evidence Suggesting Oat Consumption May Be Harmful. One recent study found that while the moderate consumption of oats did not shorten or blunt the villi of the small intestine, it did result in a significant increase in intraepithelial lymphocytes, which are white blood cells found inside the lining of the small intestine.

Lymphocytes are present wherever and whenever there is inflammation in the body, so the increase indicated a possible immune system reaction. An increase in intraepithelial lymphocytes is considered one of the first signs of mucosal damage in celiac disease.

Another study found that oats did not harm the intestinal mucosa of most—but not all—study participants. One study participant out of nineteen developed villous atrophy (blunting of the intestinal villi) and rash (the patient had dermatitis herpetiformis) while consuming oats. When oats were removed from the patient's diet, the rash resolved, and villi returned to a near-normal appearance. When oats were reintroduced, the patient again developed a rash and villous atrophy.

This finding, that one study participant appeared to be negatively affected by oats, prompted a group of researchers to further investigate the possibility of oat intolerance among some persons with celiac disease. They studied the intestinal mucosa of three patients who had previously developed mucosal inflammation while consuming oats. When biopsy tissue of the intestinal mucosa of these patients was exposed to avenin—the prolamin protein found in oats—in a test tube, researchers were able to identify lymphocytes made specifically in response to avenin. The investigators concluded that some persons with celiac disease have lymphocytes in their mucosa that can react with this oat protein and cause mucosal inflammation.

It is important to keep in mind that the number of people harmed by oats appears to be very small. Nonetheless, if you wish to add uncontaminated oats to your diet, it is important to monitor yourself for any new symptoms. (But keep in mind that oats are high in fiber, and fiber may cause gastrointestinal symptoms unrelated to celiac disease.) You also may want to discuss with your physician whether periodic serological testing would be useful. Additionally, if you are newly diagnosed with celiac disease, you may want to wait to add oats to your diet until *after* you are stabilized on a gluten-free diet.

Gluten Contamination of Oats

Another area of concern with oats is contamination with wheat, barley, or rye. According to oat millers, oats may be contaminated with one or more of these grains when they arrive at the mill. Oats are frequently grown in rotation with wheat and other grains—one year wheat is grown, the next year oats are grown, and so on. Depending upon the previous year's crop, there will likely be some foreign grain growing in the oat field, which will then be harvested along with the oats. In addition, oats may become contaminated with other grains during transport from field to mill, because shippers use railcars or trailers that may contain foreign grain from a prior load. While oats may undergo thorough cleaning at the mill and pass through sizing equipment to remove foreign grain, they nonetheless may still contain small amounts of wheat or other gluten-containing grains particularly if the grains have similar sizes.

Research on the Gluten Contamination of Commercial Oats. Relatively little information is available on the gluten contamination of commercial oats in the United States. In a study I conducted and published in 2004, twelve containers of oats (four lots taken from each of three brands—Quaker, Country Choice, and McCann's) were assessed for contamination with wheat, barley, or rye. Gluten contamination ranged from less than 3 parts per million of gluten to 1,807 parts per million. Under the Food and Drug Administration's proposed ruling for use of the term *gluten free* on food labels, gluten-free foods, including oats, must contain less than 20 parts per million of gluten. Only three of the twelve containers analyzed would be considered gluten free under this ruling and under the Draft Revised Codex Standard for Foods for Special Dietary Use for Persons Intolerant to Gluten.

In another study, published in 2006, 108 oat samples from Europe, Canada, and the United States were assessed for contamination with wheat, barley, and rye. Again, gluten contamination was substantial, with 61 percent having gluten contamination over 200 parts per million.

Gluten-Free Oats

At least five manufacturers in North America (Gluten Free Oats, Cream Hill Estates, Gifts of Nature, Bob's Red Mill, and Only Oats) produce gluten-free oats as determined through independent testing conducted by the Gluten Free Certification Organization and the Food Allergy Research and Resource Program. These manufacturers are doing this through carefully monitored growing, harvesting, and processing procedures. For more information on these oat companies, see their websites: glutenfree oats.com, pureoats.com, giftsofnature.net, bobsredmill.com, and onlyoats.com.

Recommendations for Oat Consumption

The question of whether oats should be consumed is not as easy to answer as many persons with celiac disease would like. Persons with celiac disease may want to consider the following points when deciding about oat consumption:

* For most adults and children with celiac disease, uncontaminated oats appear safe to consume in moderation (approximately ½ cup of dry rolled oats or ¼ cup of dry steel-cut oats per day).
* Some with celiac disease appear unable to tolerate even uncontaminated oats.
* Cross-contamination of oats with wheat, barley, or rye is a concern.
* Small amounts of gluten contamination in gluten-free processed foods may be inevitable. However, the ques-

tion is one of degree—what amount of contamination is acceptable.

❖ The Draft Revised Codex Standard for Foods for Special Dietary Use for Persons Intolerant to Gluten of the Codex Alimentarius Commission states that gluten-free foods may contain no more than 20 milligrams per kilogram of gluten (20 parts per million).

❖ According to the FDA's proposed rule on use of the term *gluten free* on food labels, oats may bear a "gluten-free" claim as long as they contain less than 20 parts per million of gluten. However, this amount may be changed before this rule is finalized.

❖ Brands of oats are now on the market that have been tested and consistently found to be gluten free as defined by both Codex and FDA.

When assessing whether or not to include a particular oat product in your diet, it is important to understand what tests were used to determine its gluten-free status. Tests for gluten contamination are not created equal; some are better than others. At present, the best available test for gluten contamination of oats is the R5 ELISA. This assay has a limit of detection of 3 parts per million of gluten and a limit of quantification of 5 parts per million of gluten. It has been endorsed by Codex as the method for determining gluten content of gluten-free foods and is tentatively being considered by the FDA to help enforce its regulations on "gluten-free" labeling.

To find out how a particular product was tested, call the company's customer service number or visit its website.

In My Opinion

In my opinion, oats containing less than 20 parts per million of gluten—the limit proposed by the FDA—are safe for almost all persons with celiac disease to eat. At the present time, I recommend purchasing oats only from manufacturers that document through R5 ELISA testing the level of gluten in their products. Be forewarned, however, that ordering products from these companies is expensive, and the products are not yet widely available in retail stores. However, if you miss your oats, the cost of these products may be worth it. As an added bonus, oats are quite nutritious, containing 4 grams of dietary fiber per half cup of dry rolled oats.

3

Identifying Gluten-Free Products

Probably the most difficult problem faced by celiac patients is determining whether or not they should eat certain processed packaged foods offered for sale at the retail level.

—J. A. Campbell, Canadian food and nutrition consultant and author of numerous articles on celiac disease and the gluten-free diet, 1987

THANKS TO CHANGES in food-labeling laws, it has become much easier to determine whether a food product is gluten free. These changes have certainly resulted in fewer phone calls to food manufacturers. The information in this chapter will help you determine whether a product is free of wheat, barley, rye, and oats (unless gluten free).

Ingredient Labeling of Food Products

Most of the time, you can tell whether a food contains wheat, barley, rye, or oats by reading the ingredient list found on the food label. In many cases, ingredients that are sources of these grains will be obvious because the ingredient name will contain the words *wheat, barley, rye,* or *oats.* Sometimes, however, the ingredient name does not contain these words. For detailed information on specific ingredients, see Appendix B.

Labeling of Wheat Ingredients

In the United States, most of the time, if a food or an ingredient found in a food is wheat or contains protein from wheat, the word *wheat* will be present on the food label. This is the result of the Food Allergen Labeling and Consumer Protection Act of 2004 (FALCPA).

One exception is food labeled before FALCPA went into effect (January 1, 2006). However, as time passes, you are less likely to come across a product packaged before January 1, 2006.

Another exception is food regulated by the U.S. Department of Agriculture (USDA)—namely, meat products, poultry products, and egg products. The labeling of USDA-regulated foods is explained later in this chapter.

The Food Allergen Labeling and Consumer Protection Act

The Food Allergen Labeling and Consumer Protection Act of 2004 is an amendment to a federal law (the Federal Food, Drug, and Cosmetic Act) that, among other things, regulates the labeling of food. Even though it does not specifically address gluten, it does address wheat, and that is a big help to anyone who can't eat gluten. FALCPA requires that labels of all packaged food regulated by the Food and Drug Administration and labeled on or after January 1, 2006, clearly state when a food or an ingredient found in a food is or contains protein from one of eight major allergens, including wheat. The seven other major allergens covered under FALCPA are milk, eggs, fish, crustacean shellfish, tree nuts (such as almonds, cashews, and pecans), peanuts, and soybeans.

Under FALCPA, if an ingredient in a food product is wheat or contains protein derived from wheat, the food manufacturer has two alternatives for declaring wheat on the food label:

1. The word *wheat* can be stated parenthetically immediately after the ingredient that is or contains protein from wheat. For example, if farina is an ingredient, it may be listed as "farina (wheat)" in the ingredient list.
2. The word *wheat* also can be included in a separate "Contains" statement immediately following the ingredient list. For example, after the ingredient list on a package, you may find the statement *Contains wheat.*

Manufacturers may choose one or the other alternative, so if the label has no "Contains" statement, you must read the ingredient list looking for the word *wheat*.

There is one exception to these labeling alternatives. If the word *wheat* is already present in the ingredient list, then the word *wheat* would not have to be stated again. For example, the ingredient list would not read, "wheat, farina (wheat)." It would simply read, "wheat, farina," and any other ingredients.

Keep in mind the bottom line. If an FDA-regulated food product contains protein from wheat, the word *wheat* must be clearly stated on the food label. If you don't see the word *wheat*, the product does not contain wheat protein. For a sample label on a product containing wheat, see Appendix B.

Wheat Ingredients in FDA-Regulated Foods

The FDA regulates all domestic and foreign packaged foods sold in the United States except meat, poultry, and egg products. FDA-regulated packaged foods include conventional foods, medical foods, dietary supplements, and infant formula. In addition, *prepackaged* foods labeled for sale at restaurants, delis, supermarkets, and other retailers must comply with FALCPA requirements. Raw agricultural commodities in their natural state, such as fruits and vegetables, are not considered packaged foods and are not subject to FALCPA requirements.

All ingredients found in FDA-regulated packaged foods must comply with FALCPA requirements. Therefore, if a flavoring contains protein from wheat, wheat must be declared on the food label and cannot be included under the collective term *flavoring*. If a seasoning mix or spice blend contains protein from wheat, wheat must be declared on the food label as well. Likewise, if an incidental additive, such as a processing aid, contains protein from wheat, wheat must be declared on the food label.

Note: If modified food starch, dextrin, caramel color, maltodextrin, or glucose syrup is listed in the ingredient list of an FDA-regulated food product and the word *wheat* is not included in the ingredient list or in a separate "Contains" statement, these ingredients do not contain wheat protein.

Wheat Ingredients in USDA-Regulated Foods

You have to be more vigilant when considering USDA-regulated foods, such as meat or poultry products, than with FDA-regulated foods. While all FDA-regulated packaged foods will include the word *wheat* on the food label if there is wheat protein in the product, at the present time, labels of USDA-regulated products need only list the common or usual names of ingredients containing wheat. However, the Food Safety and Inspection Service of the USDA is in the process of developing regulations for labeling of food allergens on meat, poultry, and egg products. In the meantime, the USDA encourages manufacturers to list food allergens on product labels. Regardless, it is still important to be able to identify possible "hidden" sources of wheat protein on USDA food labels.

If the food label of a USDA-regulated product includes any of the following ingredients, the food product contains wheat:

* Flour (unless, of course, the word *flour* is preceded by a descriptor such as corn, rice, or buckwheat)
* White flour
* Plain flour
* Enriched flour
* Phosphated flour
* Self-rising flour
* Graham flour
* Durum flour
* Farina
* Semolina

In addition, the following ingredients may be made from wheat starch or wheat starch hydrolysates (wheat starch that has been partially broken down):

* Modified food starch
* Dextrin
* Maltodextrin
* Caramel
* Glucose syrup

For detailed information on these ingredients, see Appendix B.

Note: It is very important to stress that while caramel, dextrin, glucose syrup, maltodextrin, and modified food starch may be made from wheat starch or wheat starch hydrolysates, according to the results of inquiries originally submitted by *Gluten-Free Living* magazine to ingredient manufacturers in the United States, manufacturers are much more likely to use cornstarch. Nonetheless, ingredient manufacturers exist worldwide, and U.S.-based food manufacturers may outsource some of the ingredients in their food products. While foreign ingredient manufacturers must comply with U.S. regulations, they may not always use cornstarch. For example, in Europe, these ingredients are more likely to be made from wheat starch.

Science Class

You may be wondering why ingredients that may be made from wheat starch hydrolysates, such as caramel, dextrin, maltodextrin, and glucose syrup, are even an issue in celiac disease. Theoretically, these ingredients should not contain protein. However, because the starch and protein components of grain cannot be completely separated, some residual protein remains in the starch. Remember, this is why there is so much controversy surrounding the use of wheat starch.

However, because some ingredients that may be made from wheat starch hydrolysates—namely wheat-based glucose syrup and wheat-based maltodextrin—contain such small amounts of gluten, they have been exempted from having to be declared as allergenic ingredients on food labels in Europe by the European Food Safety Authority. Also, keep in mind that in the United States under FALCPA, if any ingredient made from wheat starch contains wheat protein, wheat must be declared on the label of an FDA-regulated food.

In addition, under the FDA's proposed ruling regarding use of the term *gluten free* on food labels, (a complete explanation of this proposed ruling is provided later in this chapter), ingredients that have been processed to remove gluten, such as wheat starch, modified food starch made from wheat, and wheat starch hydrolysates, may be included as ingredients in foods labeled gluten free as long as their use in the food product does not result in the product having 20 parts per million or more gluten. So, while ingredients such as caramel, glucose syrup, and maltodextrin may be made from wheat starch hydrolysates, they may contain such small amounts of gluten that their use in a product still allows the product to be labeled gluten free.

Once the FDA ruling is finalized, you may see products labeled gluten free that contain wheat starch and wheat starch hydrolysates. If you wish to consume only wheat-free, gluten-free products, read the label, looking for the words *wheat* in the ingredient list and in the "Contains" statement. If wheat is not listed on the label of a gluten-free product, that product is free of wheat protein. Keep in mind, however, that if a product labeled gluten free does contain wheat starch or wheat starch hydrolysates, the product by definition contains less than 20 parts per million of gluten—a very small amount.

In My Opinion

In my opinion, if the only suspect ingredient(s) in a USDA-regulated food is maltodextrin, glucose syrup, or caramel, the food is safe for people with celiac disease to consume. Even if the source of the ingredient is wheat starch, the amount of gluten in the food product is likely very low. I would recommend continuing to avoid USDA-regulated foods containing the ingredients modified food starch and dextrin if the sources of these ingredients are not named (unless of course the product is labeled gluten free).

Barley Ingredients

FALCPA does not include barley, so it is important to be able to identify possible sources of "hidden" barley protein on food labels.

Some terms may be used on a food label in place of the word *barley*. If the label includes any of the following ingredients, the food contains barley unless the label states otherwise:

* Malt
* Malt syrup
* Malt extract
* Malt flavoring

Also, if an FDA-regulated food product contains the ingredients "natural flavor" or "caramel," there is a very small chance that these ingredients might be sources of barley. Also, there is a very small chance that if a USDA-regulated food product contains the ingredient "caramel," it might be a source of barley. It is important to note, however, that while malt may be used as a flavoring agent, it will most likely be listed as "malt flavoring" in the ingredient list and not included under the collective term *flavoring*. Caramel usually is not made from malt syrup; it is most likely made from corn.

Rye Ingredients

While FALCPA does not include rye, it is likely to be named in an ingredient list. It is possible that rye could be a "hidden" ingredient in a natural flavor of an FDA-regulated food. However, foods that would typically include rye flavoring (for example, bread products) are likely to be gluten-containing foods that you wouldn't be eating anyway.

Oat Ingredients

Products containing oats as an ingredient should not be eaten unless the product is from one of the manufacturers producing gluten-free oats. For more information on oats, see Chapter 2.

Contacting Manufacturers

If after reading the food label you still have a question about whether a product is gluten free, contact the manufacturer and ask. An address, website, or phone number generally is provided on the packaging.

"Gluten-Free" Labeling of Food Products

Finally, the United States is about to have a legal definition of the term gluten free on food labels. This ruling has been a long time in coming and should make life easier for all people with celiac disease. The information provided in this section explains what the "gluten-free" label will mean in the United States.

When this book went to press, there were no specific FDA regulations in place regarding use of the term *gluten free* on food labels. Currently, if a product is labeled gluten free, it generally means that it does not contain any ingredients made from wheat, barley, or rye (and usually oats). However, under the Food Allergen Labeling and Consumer Protection Act of 2004, the Food and Drug Administration must issue a rule regarding the definition and voluntary use of the term *gluten free* for labeling purposes by August 2008. A proposed rule has already been released.

The FDA's Rule for "Gluten-Free" Labeling

A proposed rule for the use of the term *gluten free* for food-labeling purposes was released by the FDA in January 2007. The FDA is proposing that a food product may be labeled gluten free if it does not contain any of the following:

❖ An ingredient that is any species of the grains wheat, barley, rye, or crossbred varieties of these grains

What this means: If a food product contains any type of rye, barley, or wheat, including spelt, einkorn, emmer, kamut, and durum, it may not be labeled gluten free. Likewise, if it contains triticale (a cross between wheat and rye), it may not be labeled gluten free. Conversely, all other grains, including oats, may be included in foods labeled gluten free. However, all other grain products, including oat products, labeled gluten free must contain less than 20 ppm of gluten. Because most oats are likely to be contaminated with wheat, barley, and/or rye, the labels of gluten-free oat products may not imply that all oats are gluten free.

❖ An ingredient that is derived from one of these grains that has not been processed to remove gluten

What this means: Forms of rye, barley, and wheat that have not been processed to remove protein—including wheat bran, wheat germ, cracked wheat, crushed wheat, hydrolyzed wheat protein, farina, semolina, graham flour, malt, malt syrup, and malt extract—may not be labeled gluten free.

❖ An ingredient that is derived from one of these grains that has been processed to remove gluten but use of the ingredient results in the presence of 20 ppm or more of gluten in the final food product

What this means: Products may not be labeled gluten free if they contain forms of rye, barley, and wheat, such as wheat starch, wheat-based modified food starch, and wheat starch hydrolysates (wheat-based dextrin, wheat-based glucose syrup), that have been processed to remove protein but whose use in a food product results in it containing 20 ppm or more of gluten. Conversely, wheat starch and wheat starch hydrolysates may be used as ingredients in foods labeled gluten free if their use results in the final food product containing less than 20 ppm of gluten.

❖ Twenty parts per million or more of gluten

What this means: No food product, regardless of what it contains, may be labeled gluten free if it contains 20 ppm or more of gluten.

Keep in mind that the information presented here is from the FDA's *proposed* rule. Facets of this rule may change when the final version is released in 2008.

"Gluten-free" labeling is voluntary. The lack of a statement on the label that a product is gluten free doesn't mean that it isn't. In fact, labels on foods that are inherently gluten free, such as milk, may not make a "gluten-free" claim unless the statement makes it clear that all foods of that type are gluten free. For example, a label could say, "Milk, a gluten-free food," or, "All milk is gluten free."

Why Gluten-Free Foods Are Allowed to Contain Gluten

In an ideal world, gluten-free food would not contain any gluten. However, there are reasons why a zero-gluten ruling is not feasible. First of all, there is no way to enforce such a rule, because there is no test available that can test to zero gluten. The most sensitive validated test available today is the R5 ELISA. Its limit of detection (the point at which gluten can be detected) is 3 ppm of gluten, and its limit of quantification (the point at which the amount of gluten can be quantified) is 5 ppm of gluten. Also, despite food manufacturers' best intentions, it is difficult to guarantee zero gluten, because there is always a chance (however low) of contamination.

That said, less than 20 ppm of gluten is a very low threshold. To make sure that this level is met, manufacturers will have to do everything possible to ensure the purity of the ingredients used in their products and eliminate potential sources of contamination in the manufacturing process. As a result, many (if not most) products labeled gluten free will undoubtedly contain less than 20 ppm of gluten. Rest assured that products labeled gluten free will be safe for you to eat.

Gluten-Free Foods That Contain Wheat

Once the "gluten-free" labeling rule takes effect, you may very well find foods labeled gluten free that also include the word *wheat* in the ingredient list or in the "Contains" statement. This is because the FDA may allow wheat starch and wheat starch hydrolysates to be used as ingredients in foods labeled gluten free (as long as the final food product contains less than 20 ppm of gluten). If you want to avoid ingredients containing wheat protein, choose products that do not contain the word *wheat* on the food label. Remember, under FALCPA, products containing wheat protein must be clearly labeled.

Science Class

One of the issues surrounding "gluten-free" labeling of food is the lack of standardized testing for gluten determination. At the present time, different organizations may use different methods to test for gluten. The FDA, in its proposed ruling, is tentatively considering the R5 ELISA. This is the same test endorsed by the Codex Alimentarius Commission. In addition to the R5 ELISA, other tests are available in the United States for gluten determination, including what is referred to as the omega-gliadin ELISA. This ELISA, while still used, is no longer considered state of the art.

When evaluating different programs and what their gluten-free symbols mean, it is important to know what test is being used to assess gluten content. If you would like more information about the tests used by the Celiac Sprue Association and Gluten-Free Certification Organization to assess the gluten content of the foods they certify, contact them and ask. Contact information is provided on their websites (csaceliacs.org and gfco.org).

Other Gluten-Free Symbols on Food Packaging

Besides the FDA requirements for "gluten-free" labeling, you may see two symbols on package labels identifying food products as gluten free. One is a symbol of the Gluten-Free Certification Organization (GFCO), a program run by the Gluten Intolerance Group. According to the group's website (gfco.org), a GFCO mark on a food product "assures that the product contains less than 10 ppm gluten (5 ppm gliadin) and similar proteins from rye and barley as measured by using testing methods that are accepted for gluten testing by analytical associations such as the Association of Analytical Communities (AOAC), testing researchers and other such agencies."

The second symbol, the CSA Seal of Recognition, is a program run by the Celiac Sprue Association. According to the

Used with permission of the Gluten-Free Certification Organization, a program of the Gluten Intolerance Group of North America.

Used with permission of the Celiac Sprue Association.

association's website (csaceliacs.org), requirements for obtaining the seal include "ingredient review and verification by testing to assure products are free of wheat, barley, rye and oats" and "provision of written facility procedures and on-site facility audits to assure that procedures are in place to control any cross or outside contamination in processing and packaging."

If you see either of these two labels on a food product, rest assured that the product meets the requirements set by the issuing organization. For more information on these two programs, visit their websites.

Other Products That Contain Gluten

Gluten may be found in many products, ranging from the obvious (food) to the less obvious, such as medication. This section provides an overview of the categories of products that may contain gluten.

Processed Foods That Contain Gluten

All processed foods can potentially contain wheat, barley, rye, or contaminated oats. Therefore, it is extremely important that you read the ingredient lists of all processed foods to look for sources of these grains. Manufacturers may change the ingredients they use to make a product, so it is important to check labels frequently, if not every time you shop.

Processed foods that contain, or often contain, sources of harmful grain include the following examples:

* Bouillon cubes
* Broth (beef, chicken, and vegetable)
* Brown-rice syrup
* Candy
* Cold cuts, hot dogs, salami, sausage
* Communion wafers
* French fries
* Gravy
* Imitation fish (for instance, surimi)
* Licorice
* Malt vinegar (**Note:** Whereas malt vinegar, which is made from barley malt, is not gluten free, other vinegars—including distilled vinegar, cider vinegar, wine vinegar, and balsamic vinegar—are gluten free.)
* Malted milk
* Matzo
* Rice mixes
* Sauces
* Seasoned meat and poultry
* Seasoned tempeh
* Seasoned tofu
* Seasoned tortilla chips or potato chips
* Self-basting turkey
* Soups
* Soy milk
* Soy sauce
* Tamari sauce

- ❖ Teriyaki sauce
- ❖ Vegetables in sauce
- ❖ Vegetarian "burgers" and "hot dogs"

Communion Wafers. In general, Communion wafers are made from wheat. However, low-gluten and gluten-free varieties may be special-ordered. Canon Law dictates that Communion wafers used to celebrate the Eucharist must contain some amount of wheat. The Benedictine Sisters of Perpetual Adoration have developed wheat-starch-based low-gluten Communion wafers that comply with Canon Law. Rice-based Communion wafers are available from Ener-G Foods, Inc.

In My Opinion

Low-gluten Communion wafers made from wheat starch are, I believe, safe for persons with celiac disease to use to celebrate Mass. The wafers made by the Benedictine Sisters reportedly contain 0.01 percent gluten, which is equivalent to 100 parts per million of gluten. While I normally would not endorse the regular consumption of food containing this proportion of gluten, we also need to consider the total amount of food consumed. The smaller of the two breads weighs only 0.04 gram. Each wafer therefore contains only 0.004 milligram of gluten, which is an exceedingly small amount. The weekly use of one very small wafer containing this level of gluten is not going to pose much risk to most people with celiac disease.

Matzo. Matzo is generally made from wheat. However, a rabbi in England has developed an oat-based matzo that is advertised as gluten free.

For more information on Communion wafers and matzo, see the resource lists in Appendix A.

Alcoholic Beverages

If, before your diagnosis with celiac disease, you enjoyed a glass of wine with dinner or a beer with your pizza, you may find this section helpful. While some alcoholic beverages contain protein from wheat, barley, and rye, most do not. This section explains the various classes of alcohol.

Beer. Beer, lager, ale, porter, stout, and pilsner are fermented alcoholic beverages produced at least in part from malt or a substitute for malt. If these beverages are made from wheat, barley, or rye, they are not gluten free. If these beverages are made using another grain but contain barley malt, they are not gluten free. The good news for many is that several sources of gluten-free beer are now available in the United States. For more information, please see the resources listed in Appendix A.

Other malt-based beverages, such as some wine coolers, hard lemonade, and some flavored hard ciders, contain gluten. True hard cider, however, is gluten free.

Science Class

Unless you are a brewer, vintner, or distiller, you may not realize why distillation *is* compatible and fermentation in general *is not* compatible with a gluten-free diet. Alcoholic beverages are either fermented or distilled. Fermented and distilled beverages are made by first converting starch or sugar from a food source (for example, grapes, wheat, or potato) to alcohol, using yeast. With fermented beverages, such as beer, the liquid removed from the mash (the mixture of starting materials) is boiled. If a gluten-containing grain is one of the food sources used to make the mash, the liquid removed from the mash is not gluten free. With distilled beverages, such as vodka, the liquid removed from the mash is not only boiled but also distilled. Distillation is used to increase the alcohol content of the beverage. When the liquid is boiled, the vapor is "captured" and cooled. The resulting liquid is called the distillate. Distillation separates substances that are volatile (meaning they vaporize) from less volatile substances. Protein is not volatile and does not vaporize. Consequently, even if wheat, barley, or rye was used to make a distilled alcoholic beverage, gluten-containing proteins will not be found in the final distillate.

Sake. Sake should be gluten free. While sake is a fermented beverage, it is made from polished rice and koji mold. Koji mold is grown on rice that has been "contaminated" with koji spores. While koji mold can be grown on other grains, including those that contain gluten, this is unlikely for a rice-based beverage.

Wine. Wine is gluten free. While wine is a fermented beverage, it is made from grapes or other fruit. Fortified wines also are gluten free. These beverages, such as sherry, port, and vermouth, are simply wines with added brandy or another distilled alcohol.

Spirits. Pure spirits—distilled alcohol from fruit, sugar, or grain—are gluten free. While grain alcohol, such as vodka, gin, and whiskey, may be made from gluten-containing grains, the process of distillation prevents any protein from ending up in the final distillate. Some alcoholic beverages, including rum, may have caramel added as a coloring agent. If you have concerns about caramel (and you probably shouldn't, because it is most likely made from corn), contact the manufacturer. In addition, some distilled alcoholic beverages, such as cordials and liqueurs, may have flavorings added after distillation. These flavorings are likely to be gluten free, but if you have concerns about flavorings, contact the manufacturer.

For information on the labeling of alcoholic beverages, see the website of the Bureau of Alcohol, Tobacco, Firearms, and

Explosives, atf.treas.gov. In the website's search engine, enter "alcohol labeling."

Medications and Dietary Supplements

Supplements and medications, whether sold over the counter or by prescription, may contain fillers made from gluten-containing grains. Unfortunately, prescription medications generally do not come with an ingredient list. You should speak with your pharmacist or the manufacturer about whether your medication is gluten free.

Supplements and over-the-counter medications contain a list of ingredients on their label. Labels for over-the-counter medications list both active ingredients (the ones that provide the therapeutic benefits, such as pain relief) and inactive ingredients (those that do not provide any therapeutic benefits, such as colorings and fillers).

The Food Allergen Labeling and Consumer Protection Act of 2004 applies to dietary supplements, medical foods, and infant formula. If one of these products contains protein from wheat, the word *wheat* must be included on the product's label. If you have any questions about whether a product is gluten free, you should contact the manufacturer.

Several resources are available to help you determine whether your medications are gluten free. To find a list of these, see the resources in Appendix A.

Cosmetics and Toiletries

Products that you apply to your skin and hair may be made from gluten-containing ingredients. However, you do not need to be concerned about products that you do not ingest. If products you apply to your lips (such as lipstick) or use in your mouth (such as toothpaste or mouthwash) are made using gluten-containing ingredients, you might ingest some gluten. Keep in mind that the amount of gluten in many of these products is likely to be very small, and the amount you might ingest even smaller. Nonetheless, it makes sense to use gluten-free versions of these products. Contact the manufacturer to find out if your favorite brands are gluten free.

Cross-Contamination

Bread crumbs in the butter, pasta starch in the strainer, crouton crumbs in the salad—these are just a few of the ways gluten-free foods may become contaminated with gluten-full foods. When you are trying so hard to make sure that the food you eat is free of gluten, you don't want to sabotage yourself by being lax with contamination. Use the information in this section to help decrease your chances of eating contaminated food.

Cross-contamination or cross-contact is the accidental "contamination" of a gluten-free food with a gluten-containing food. Cross-contamination can occur anywhere food is grown, harvested, manufactured, processed, or prepared, including at home and in restaurants.

Cross-Contamination at Home

Unless all food brought into your home is gluten free, there is the potential for cross-contamination. This does not mean that all food prepared in your home has to be gluten free or that certain pieces of silverware or place settings need to be designated gluten free. However, there are some steps you can take to reduce the risk of cross-contamination in your home:

❖ Store gluten-free grain foods in a separate cupboard or on separate shelves above gluten-containing grain foods. This is especially important with flours, which have a mysterious way of leaking out of bags, as well as foods such as breads and crackers, which tend to make crumbs.

❖ When baking both gluten-free and gluten-containing breads, cakes, cookies, or other foods, always prepare and bake the gluten-free item first. It is almost impossible not to spill at least some flour along the way, and it is far better to get gluten-free flour in the gluten-containing flour than the other way around.

❖ When preparing and serving both gluten-free and gluten-containing foods, use separate utensils (for example, pasta tongs, bread knives, and serving spoons).

❖ When preparing both gluten-free and gluten-containing foods, use separate preparation tools, such as cutting boards and pasta strainers. Alternatively, prepare the gluten-free product first.

❖ Clean your toaster oven, bread machine, and other appliances used for both gluten-free and gluten-containing foods after each use with gluten-containing products.

❖ Use squeeze bottles for ketchup, mustard, mayonnaise, and other condiments that are used with both gluten-free and gluten-containing products. Alternatively, make sure there is no "double dipping"—sticking a utensil back into a condiment jar after it has been used to spread the condiment on gluten-containing bread.

❖ Institute a no-double-dipping rule for other spreadables, such as butter, margarine, and cream cheese.

❖ When serving food buffet-style at your home, place the gluten-free foods together and slightly apart from the gluten-containing foods. This way, serving utensils from the gluten-free foods are less likely to get mixed up with the gluten-containing foods.

❖ When hosting a dinner party at your home, it is often easiest to make the menu entirely gluten free. That way, you know that the butter, cheese, and other items will remain free of gluten-containing bread or cracker crumbs and that mixed-up serving utensils will not cause a problem.

Cross-Contamination in Restaurants

It is easy to understand how cross-contamination could occur in a restaurant, as gluten-free and gluten-containing foods undoubtedly are prepared in the same kitchen. However, this should not prevent you from eating out. A few precautions will help reduce the risk of cross-contamination in restaurants:

❖ When ordering a salad, make sure to stress to the server that croutons should not be included.

❖ Avoid salad bars unless they are very basic and all the ingredients are gluten free. The serving utensils may have been "shared" among the various food items.

❖ When ordering french fries, check with your server to make sure breaded foods are not deep-fried in the same oil as the fries. If so, don't order the french fries. Also, make sure that the french fries are not "coated" to help them brown—these coatings usually contain flour.

❖ When ordering a grilled item, ask that a portion of the grill be cleaned for your item or that a separate pan be used.

❖ When ordering a frozen dessert, such as sorbet or ice cream, stress to the server that cookies should not be included.

In My Opinion

While it is important to strive to consume as little gluten as possible (and ideally no gluten at all), from a practical standpoint, this is likely not feasible. If you eat any processed food or food prepared in anything but a dedicated gluten-free kitchen, you are likely to consume some gluten. However, as long as you take precautions to limit cross-contamination and make sure the foods you eat are not made with any gluten-containing ingredients, I would advise sitting back, relaxing, and enjoying your meal.

Cross-Contamination of Processed Foods

The potential for contamination exists for all processed gluten-free foods, including those specially formulated to be gluten free and those that just happen to not contain any gluten.

The processed gluten-free foods that you purchase may be manufactured in one of several types of facilities, including those that manufacture only gluten-free foods or that have a separate area or room within their facility for gluten-free products, as well as those that have separate production lines for gluten-free foods. Processed gluten-free foods also may share production lines with gluten-containing foods. However, this doesn't necessarily mean these products will be contaminated. Many manufacturers have an allergen control plan in place, and all manufacturers should follow current good manufacturing practices. These practices may include thorough cleaning of shared equipment as well as timed product turnovers. If you have questions about a company's manufacturing practices, contact the company (a company address, phone number, and/or website is generally included on the food label), and ask to speak with a quality assurance representative.

4

Avoiding Nutritional Pitfalls in a Gluten-Free Diet

"Gluten-free" foodstuffs, substituting important basic foodstuffs should supply approximately the same amount of vitamins and minerals as the original foodstuffs they replace.

—Codex Committee on Nutrition and Foods for Special Dietary Uses, 1998

A GLUTEN-FREE DIET can be a nutritional powerhouse and provide you with all the nutrients necessary for a healthful diet. However, the typical gluten-free diet as generally followed in the United States may be lacking in certain nutrients, including the B vitamins thiamin, riboflavin, niacin, and folate, the minerals iron and calcium, and dietary fiber. In addition, a gluten-free diet (just like any American diet) has the potential to be high in fat, including trans and saturated fat.

Nutritional Quality of the Gluten-Free Diet

Very few studies have been conducted on the nutritional adequacy of the gluten-free diet, and to date, only one of these studies has

evaluated the diet in the United States. The U.S. study assessed
the intake of fiber, iron, calcium, and grain foods of adults with
celiac disease. Notable findings included below-recommended
intake of dietary fiber, iron, calcium, and grain foods among the
majority of female participants. In fact, recommended amounts
of fiber, iron, and calcium were consumed by only 46 percent, 44
percent, and 31 percent of women participants, respectively. The
situation was a bit better for men, but 12 percent and 37 percent
of male participants did not consume recommended amounts of
fiber and calcium, respectively. While all readers should be mind-
ful of the nutritional adequacy of their diet, women in particular
should pay close attention to their intakes of these nutrients.

The following sections will show you how to avoid the nutritional pitfalls of the gluten-free diet. Armed with this knowledge and
the delicious and nutritious recipes in Chapter 6, you can eat as well
as, if not even better than, someone with no dietary restrictions.

B Vitamins, Iron, and Dietary Fiber

Whole-grain and enriched or fortified varieties of grain food such
as bread products, pasta, and breakfast cereals contribute a significant amount of B vitamins, iron, and dietary fiber to the diets
of Americans. It may be difficult to get the nutrients you need on
a gluten-free diet because the majority of specially manufactured
gluten-free breads, pastas, and cereals are neither whole grain nor
enriched. As a result, they contain very little thiamin, riboflavin,
niacin, folate, iron, and dietary fiber, which are all crucial for
leading a healthy lifestyle.

Specially manufactured gluten-free breads, pastas, and cereals often are made from starch such as rice starch, cornstarch, and
potato starch, or refined flour such as milled rice and milled corn.
During the milling process, when a whole grain such as brown
rice is refined to make white rice, the bran and germ of the grain
are removed. Much of the vitamins, minerals, and dietary fiber
found in grains come from these portions.

In the United States, most refined wheat-based breads and pasta are voluntarily enriched with thiamin, riboflavin, niacin, folic acid (the synthetic form of folate), and iron. Enrichment means that the nutrients (with the exception of fiber) lost during the milling process are added back into the food. Also, most regular breakfast cereals are fortified with vitamins and minerals. Unfortunately, most refined, specially manufactured gluten-free breads, pastas, and breakfast cereals are neither enriched nor fortified. It is unclear why most manufacturers of gluten-free foods do not enrich their products. Perhaps the reason is simply that they are not required to. Because enrichment of refined wheat-based grain foods is voluntary in the United States, gluten-free substitutes for these products do not have to be enriched.

Historical Nuggets

- As recently as 2000, no manufacturers of specially formulated gluten-free foods available in the United States were enriching or fortifying pasta products or ready-to-eat breakfast cereal. But at present, Maple Grove Food and Beverage (Pastariso and Pastato brands) enriches a variety of pasta products, and Enjoy Life Natural Foods (Enjoy Life and Perky's brands) fortifies a variety of ready-to-eat breakfast cereals.
- In a survey of celiac disease support groups in the United States in 2000, there was no consensus on whether the grains millet and sorghum and the pseudocereals amaranth, buckwheat, and quinoa are gluten free (they are). Now these whole grains are used by several manufacturers of gluten-free foods, and you can find them in a wide variety of products.

Enriched Versus Fortified Foods. You will sometimes see the terms *enriched* and *fortified* used interchangeably when referring to food products, but they are not quite the same. In general, when the word *enriched* appears on a food label, it means that vitamins and minerals have been added back to a refined grain food that originally contained them until they were removed during the milling process. Under regulations of the Food and Drug Administration, only certain foods in the United States may be voluntarily enriched with specific vitamins and minerals. This is done in part to prevent overconsumption of a specific nutrient. Foods that may be enriched include bread, rolls, buns, flour, macaroni, noodle products, rice, cornmeal, and farina. To be labeled enriched, these products must contain certain amounts of thiamin, riboflavin, niacin, folic acid, and iron.

In addition, foods may be fortified with a wide variety of vitamins and minerals that may or may not have been found in the original food product. The amounts of specific nutrients that may be added to fortified food products may or may not be regulated, depending on the specific food and nutrient. Examples of foods that may be fortified include breakfast cereal, soy milk, orange juice, and energy bars.

Whole Grains Versus Refined Grains. To give you an idea of the nutritional differences between a whole grain and a refined grain, consider the following comparison between white- and brown-rice flour:

Nutrient Comparison: White-Rice Flour and Brown-Rice Flour			
	White-Rice Flour	Brown-Rice Flour	Percentage Difference
Amount	1 cup (158 grams)	1 cup (158 grams)	—
Calories	578	574	—
Iron (mg)	0.55	3.13	469%
Riboflavin (mg)	0.03	0.13	333%
Thiamin (mg)	0.22	0.70	218%
Niacin (mg)	4.09	10.02	145%
Dietary fiber (g)	3.8	7.3	92%
Folate (DFE*)	6.0	25.0	32%
Calcium (mg)	16.0	17.0	6%

*DFE stands for dietary folate equivalent, discussed later in this chapter.

Enriched Grains Versus Unenriched Grains. To get an idea of the nutritional differences between an unenriched and an enriched refined grain, consider the following comparison between unenriched and enriched cornmeal:

Nutrient Comparison: Unenriched Degermed Cornmeal and Enriched Degermed Cornmeal			
	Cornmeal, Unenriched	Cornmeal, Enriched	Percentage Difference
Amount	1 cup (138 grams)	1 cup (138 grams)	—
Calories	587	587	—
Iron (mg)	1.75	6.87	393%
Riboflavin (mg)	0.08	0.66	825%
Thiamin (mg)	0.22	0.98	445%
Niacin (mg)	1.59	8.44	531%
Dietary fiber (g)	6.4	6.4	—
Folate (DFE*)	48.0	549.0	1,144%
Calcium (mg)	5.0	5.0	—

*DFE stands for dietary folate equivalent, discussed later in this chapter.

As the preceding examples illustrate, whole-grain and enriched foods are more nutrient dense than refined and unenriched foods. This means they provide higher levels of nutrients for the same calorie content. The recipes in this book will give you some great ideas for cooking with a variety of gluten-free whole grains.

Calcium

Some persons with celiac disease, especially those who are newly diagnosed, may have a secondary form of lactose intolerance. Lactose is a type of sugar found in milk. To be digested, it must be broken down in the small intestine by the enzyme lactase. Persons newly diagnosed with celiac disease may have low levels of lactase as a result of damage to the lining of the small intestine.

As the small intestine heals in response to a gluten-free diet, the lactose intolerance will naturally resolve. Until it does, a lactose-reduced or lactose-free diet is generally recommended.

Because individuals with lactose intolerance may avoid milk products, and because milk products are a major source of calcium in the American diet, persons with celiac disease who also are lactose intolerant may not consume enough calcium.

Fat

There is nothing inherent in a gluten-free diet that makes it more (or less) likely to be high in fat. Nonetheless, many gluten-free diets are high in fat. For overall health and well-being, persons with celiac disease should pay attention to the fat content of their diet, especially as it concerns saturated and trans fats. Any diet that contains full-fat diary products, processed snack foods, and fatty meat products may be high in unhealthful fat. You'll find out more about fat and the gluten-free diet later in this chapter.

All About Fiber

A lot of advertisements for fiber supplements give the impression that getting your fiber from food is exceedingly difficult. Well, it isn't. Fiber abounds in fruits, vegetables, legumes, and whole grains. As long as you make smart food choices—and this section will help—your diet will be naturally high in fiber.

Fiber is a carbohydrate that cannot be digested and therefore is not absorbed into the body. As a result, it travels through the digestive system and is excreted. The term *dietary fiber* describes natural fiber found in plant foods. This is the type of fiber listed in the Nutrition Facts label of the food products you buy. The term *total fiber* is defined as dietary fiber plus functional fiber. Functional fiber is fiber added to food as an ingredient, such as guar gum and xanthan gum. Functional fiber may be either synthetic (manufactured) or natural. Both dietary fiber and functional fiber are beneficial.

The amount of fiber you need varies depending upon your age, gender, and overall caloric intake. On a food package's Nutrition Facts label, the daily value of dietary fiber for adults is based on calorie consumption:

Calories Consumed	Daily Value of Dietary Fiber
2,000 per day	25 grams
2,500 per day	30 grams

The Dietary Reference Intake (DRI)—the reference value for nutrient intake established by the federal government—for total fiber is related to age and gender:

Gender and Age Group	DRI for Total Fiber
Men, 19–50 years	38 grams
Men, over 50	30 grams
Women, 19–50 years	25 grams
Women, over 50	21 grams

Fiber may play a role in prevention and treatment of diseases, especially cardiovascular disease and diabetes. Specifically, fiber may help reduce LDL cholesterol—the type of cholesterol that may form plaque along the walls of arteries—and regulate blood sugar levels. In addition, fiber helps treat and prevent constipation. Fiber softens the stool and increases its bulk. Increased fecal bulk causes the large intestine to contract, which helps move the stool through the colon.

Fiber and the Gluten-Free Diet

A gluten-free diet can contain enough fiber, but you will have to make an extra effort to choose foods that are good sources of fiber. Most Americans consume only half the recommended amounts of dietary fiber. Furthermore, in a typical American diet, grain foods (typically, yeast bread, ready-to-eat cereal, pasta, and flour) contribute over 25 percent of an adult's intake of fiber. Many people with celiac disease do not consume the recommended number of servings of grain foods. Processed grain foods that are included in a gluten-free diet may not be good sources of fiber—many gluten-free grain foods are made from refined flours and starches, which contain very little fiber.

Adding Fiber to Your Diet

All plant foods, including fruits, vegetables, legumes, and whole grains, contain fiber. Therefore, as you will see from the suggestions provided here, it is very easy to add fiber to your diet. There is one word of caution, however: it is best to add fiber to your diet gradually. A rapid increase in fiber intake can cause stomach and intestinal distress, including gas, bloating, and diarrhea—conditions that sometimes may be wrongly associated with a gluten reaction. But if you increase fiber intake gradually, you reduce the chance of developing these symptoms.

High-Fiber Fruits. According to *Dietary Guidelines for Americans, 2005*, the most recent edition of a guide published jointly by the U.S. Department of Health and Human Services and Department of Agriculture, a person requiring 2,000 calories a day should consume 2 cups (four servings) of fruit each day. A ½-cup serving of fruit is equivalent to ½ cup of fresh fruit or ¼ cup of dried fruit.

While all fruits contain fiber, some are better sources than others. The following table identifies some of the best fruit sources of fiber per serving.

Fruit Sources of Fiber Containing at Least 2.5 Grams of Fiber per Serving		
Food	**Serving Size**	**Dietary Fiber**
Raspberries (raw)	½ cup	4.0 grams
Blackberries (raw)	½ cup	3.8 grams
Figs (dried)	¼ cup (approximately 4 figs)	3.7 grams
Dates, chopped	¼ cup	3.6 grams
Prunes	¼ cup (approximately 5 prunes)	3.1 grams
Pear	½ cup (approximately ½ medium pear)	2.8 grams
Kiwi	½ cup (approximately 1 kiwi)	2.7 grams

High-Fiber Vegetables. According to *Dietary Guidelines for Americans*, a person requiring 2,000 calories a day should consume 2½ cups (five servings) of vegetables each day. A ½-cup serving of vegetables is equivalent to ½ cup of cooked vegetables, ½ cup of raw vegetables, or 1 cup of raw leafy green vegetables.

While all vegetables contain fiber, some are better sources than others. The following table identifies some of the best vegetable sources of fiber per serving.

Vegetable Sources of Fiber Containing at Least 2.5 Grams of Fiber per Serving		
Food	**Serving Size**	**Dietary Fiber**
Artichoke hearts (cooked)	½ cup	4.5 grams
Green peas (frozen, cooked)	½ cup	4.4 grams
Spinach (frozen, cooked)	½ cup	3.5 grams
Squash, winter (cooked)	½ cup	2.9 grams
Parsnips (cooked)	½ cup	2.8 grams
Broccoli (cooked)	½ cup	2.6 grams
Turnip greens (cooked)	½ cup	2.5 grams

Legumes: Dried Beans, Peas, and Lentils. According to *Dietary Guidelines for Americans*, a person requiring 2,000 calories a day should consume 3 cups of legumes (dried beans, peas, and lentils) a week. When you think of beans, you may think only of whole beans, but a variety of products are made from beans, including flour, pasta, and breakfast cereal. Appendix C lists manufacturers of gluten-free foods made from beans. Also, see Chapter 6 for recipes using beans.

Dietary Fiber Content of Selected Legumes

Food	Serving Size	Dietary Fiber
Navy beans (cooked)	½ cup	9.6 grams
Split peas (cooked)	½ cup	8.1 grams
Lentils (cooked)	½ cup	7.8 grams
Pinto beans (cooked)	½ cup	7.7 grams
Black beans (cooked)	½ cup	7.5 grams
Kidney beans, red (cooked)	½ cup	6.5 grams
Baked beans (cooked)	½ cup	5.2 grams

Gluten-Free Whole Grains. According to *Dietary Guidelines for Americans*, a person requiring 2,000 calories a day should consume six 1-ounce-equivalent servings of grain foods daily, and at least three of these servings should be whole grains. As I mentioned earlier in this chapter, whole grains contain all three components of the grain kernel: the outer fiber-rich bran layer, the nutrient-rich germ, and the starchy endosperm. Refined grains contain only the endosperm.

Science Class

Oats contain a type of dietary fiber called beta-glucan soluble fiber. Consuming at least 3 grams of this type of fiber from oats each day may reduce the risk of coronary heart disease by decreasing blood levels of cholesterol. The evidence supporting the cholesterol-lowering effects of oats prompted the Food and Drug Administration to allow a health claim for oats on food labels. Three grams of soluble fiber are found in 60 grams (¾ cup) of dry rolled oats. This amount is slightly more than the moderate amount (50 grams) of oats recommended for consumption for persons with celiac disease.

If you are considering adding this grain to your diet, please read the section on oats (Chapter 2). If you do eat oats, they can be a great source of fiber, but be careful not to overdo it.

Gluten-free whole grains include popcorn, brown rice, wild rice, whole-grain corn, buckwheat, amaranth, millet, quinoa, sorghum, oats, and teff. Look for products where one of these grains is listed as the first ingredient. Some gluten-free grain foods are made from a mixture of whole grains and refined grains. Appendix C lists manufacturers of gluten-free products made with whole grains.

Use the nutrition label to choose products with at least 2.5 grams of dietary fiber per serving. One ounce (approximately 28 grams) of a gluten-free grain food is equivalent to one serving. For example, according to the food label on a particular brand of packaged brown-rice cakes, one rice cake weighs 9 grams. Therefore, a 1-ounce-equivalent serving of rice cakes would be approximately three rice cakes. See Appendix B for tips on using the Nutrition Facts label.

Dietary Fiber Content of Selected Gluten-Free Whole Grains and Flours		
Food	**Serving Size**	**Dietary Fiber**
Teff grain (raw)	¼ cup (45 grams)	6.0 grams
Amaranth seed (raw)	¼ cup (49 grams)	4.5 grams
Buckwheat groats (raw)	¼ cup (41 grams)	4.2 grams
Millet grits (raw)	¼ cup (50 grams)	4.2 grams
Popcorn	1 ounce (approximately 2½ cups)	4.1 grams
Millet flour	¼ cup (30 grams)	4.0 grams
Oats (raw)	¼ cup (40 grams)	4.0 grams
Teff flour	¼ cup (30 grams)	4.0 grams
Amaranth flour	¼ cup (30 grams)	3.0 grams
Buckwheat flour	¼ cup (30 grams)	3.0 grams
Sorghum, white (raw)	¼ cup (48 grams)	3.0 grams
Sorghum flour	¼ cup (34 grams)	3.0 grams
Quinoa seed (raw)	¼ cup (43 grams)	2.5 grams
Whole-grain corn flour	¼ cup (29 grams)	2.1 grams
Brown rice (cooked)	½ cup	1.8 grams
Brown-rice flour	¼ cup (40 grams)	1.8 grams
Wild rice (cooked)	½ cup	1.5 grams

All About Calcium

Many people with celiac disease do not consume enough calcium, a mineral found in the body primarily in the bones and teeth. To emphasize that point, it's worth repeating some data I mentioned earlier in this chapter: in a study of the nutritional intakes of people with celiac disease in the United States, 69 percent of women and 39 percent of men did not consume recommended amounts of calcium. Regardless of whether you drink milk, there really is no reason to have low calcium intake; plenty of calcium-fortified foods are available, as well as foods other than milk that contain calcium.

The amount of calcium you need varies by age. For men and women who are nineteen to fifty years old, the Dietary Reference Intake (DRI) for calcium is 1,000 milligrams. For men and women over fifty, the DRI for calcium is 1,200 milligrams.

Calcium is important for the formation and maintenance of bone. At any given time in our bodies, new bone is being formed, and old bone is being broken down. This process occurs throughout our life, although at different rates. Until around the age of thirty, new bone is formed at a faster rate than old bone is broken down. This is the time when we are developing our peak bone mass—as much bone as we will ever have. Then, from about age thirty to fifty, bone formation and breakdown occur at approximately the same rate. As we age (and as women reach menopause), the breakdown of bone starts to occur faster than the formation of new bone. The goal throughout our lives is to maximize bone mass and minimize bone loss. Calcium plays an important role in both of these processes.

Osteoporosis and Celiac Disease

Osteoporosis, as well as other, less severe forms of bone disease, may be a complication of long-term untreated celiac disease, because the body cannot properly absorb calcium and vitamin D. (Vitamin D enhances the absorption of calcium and is necessary for the proper formation of bone.) Osteoporosis is a bone disease characterized by low bone mass and structural changes within the bone that weaken it and increase the risk of fracture. There are several risk factors for osteoporosis, including inadequate calcium intake and poor absorption of calcium. Before diagnosis, people with celiac disease often experience malabsorption as a result of damage to the lining of the small intestine. Consequently, their bone mineral density or peak bone mass may not be optimal. Once you are diagnosed with celiac disease and your issues with malabsorption have been resolved on a gluten-free diet, it is important that you consume recommended amounts of calcium to help improve your bone mineral density.

Calcium and the Gluten-Free Diet

The good news is that, while people with untreated celiac disease may not absorb enough calcium, there is nothing about a gluten-free diet that should limit calcium intake. The primary sources of calcium in the American diet—milk and cheese—are readily available to persons following a gluten-free diet. However, as mentioned earlier, many people with celiac disease have a usually temporary secondary form of lactose intolerance and cannot digest the sugar in milk products. If this describes you, there are still plenty of foods you can eat that contain calcium.

In addition, many people with celiac disease also are on other special diets, including low fat and vegetarian. If you are on such a diet, it is still possible to get all the calcium you need. The next section will help you do just that.

Adding Calcium to Your Diet

You can get enough calcium in your diet even if you follow a vegetarian or vegan diet, are lactose intolerant, follow a low-fat diet, or just don't eat dairy products. A combination of the foods listed in this section will enable you to get enough calcium in your diet while suiting your particular needs.

Milk Products. *Dietary Guidelines for Americans, 2005* recommends that adults drink 3 cups of fat-free or low-fat milk or consume the equivalent each day. One cup of milk is equivalent to 1 cup of yogurt, 1½ ounces of hard natural cheese, 2 cups of cottage cheese, 1 cup of frozen yogurt, or 1½ cups of ice cream.

Calcium Content of Selected Milk Products			
Food	**Serving Size**	**Calories**	**Calcium**
Milk, 1% low-fat	1 cup	102	290 milligrams
Milk, 2% reduced-fat	1 cup	122	285 milligrams
Yogurt, plain, low-fat	1 cup	154	448 milligrams
Yogurt, vanilla, low-fat	1 cup	208	419 milligrams
Cheddar cheese, low-fat	1½ ounces	74	176 milligrams
Ricotta cheese, part-skim	½ cup	170	335 milligrams
Cottage cheese, 2%	2 cups	407	312 milligrams
Cottage cheese, 1%	2 cups	325	276 milligrams
Ice cream, chocolate	1½ cups	428	216 milligrams
Frozen yogurt, chocolate	1 cup	221	174 milligrams

Consuming three servings of milk products each day does not have to add a lot of calories and fat to your diet if you choose low-fat products most often. For example, consuming 1 cup of 1 percent milk, 1 cup of low-fat plain yogurt, and 1½ ounces of low-fat cheddar cheese provides you with 914 milligrams of calcium (and only 330 calories).

Calcium-Fortified Foods. If you do not consume milk products, it is recommended that you consume foods fortified with calcium, such as calcium-fortified orange juice, calcium-fortified energy bars, calcium-fortified soy products, and other calcium-fortified nonmilk beverages, such as those made from rice and nuts. Some gluten-free grain foods (including breads, bagels, and granola cereals) also are fortified with calcium. Products include those made by Enjoy Life Foods and Glutino. For a listing of manufacturers of enriched and fortified gluten-free foods, please see Appendix C.

As you can see from the following table, calcium-fortified versions of soy milk and orange juice are comparable in calcium content to milk products.

Calcium Content of Calcium-Fortified and Unfortified Foods

Food	Calcium-Fortified	Unfortified
1 cup soy milk	368 milligrams	93 milligrams
1 cup orange juice	351 milligrams	27 milligrams

Other Nonmilk Foods That Are Sources of Calcium. If you do not consume milk products or calcium-fortified foods, it is especially important to eat other food sources of calcium.

Calcium Content of Selected Foods

Food	Amount	Calcium
Rhubarb (cooked)	½ cup	174 milligrams
Collards (cooked)	½ cup	133 milligrams
Soybeans (green, cooked)	½ cup	130 milligrams
Spinach (cooked)	½ cup	122 milligrams
Ocean perch (cooked)	3 ounces	116 milligrams
Soybeans (mature, cooked)	½ cup	88 milligrams
White beans (cooked)	½ cup	81 milligrams
Almonds	1 ounce (23 nuts)	75 milligrams
Trout (wild, cooked)	3 ounces	73 milligrams
Tahini	1 tablespoon	64 milligrams
Navy beans (cooked)	½ cup	63 milligrams
Great Northern beans (cooked)	½ cup	60 milligrams
Halibut (cooked)	3 ounces	51 milligrams
Molasses	1 tablespoon	41 milligrams
Pinto beans (cooked)	½ cup	39 milligrams
Chick-peas (canned)	½ cup	38 milligrams
Orange sections	½ cup (approximately 1 small orange)	38 milligrams
Broccoli (chopped, cooked)	½ cup	30 milligrams

If You Are Lactose Intolerant

If you are lactose intolerant and are following a lactose-free or lactose-reduced diet, there may be several milk products that you can consume:

❖ **Lactose-free milk:** As the name suggests, lactose-free milk contains little to no lactose. Available brands include Lactaid and Land O Lakes Dairy Ease. These products provide 300 milligrams of calcium per 1-cup serving and are available in fat-free, low-fat, and reduced-fat versions.

❖ **Hard cheese:** Cheddar and Swiss cheese contain very low amounts of lactose and may be well tolerated.

❖ **Yogurt with active, live cultures:** This product also may be tolerated, because it contains an enzyme that may help digest lactose.

If you are unable to consume enough calcium from food, you may want to talk to your dietitian or physician about taking a gluten-free calcium supplement. For a listing of manufacturers of gluten-free supplements, see Appendix A.

All About Folate

I can't stress enough the importance of consuming enough folate, especially if you are a woman capable of becoming pregnant. Adequate folate consumption is so important that in 1996 the Food and Drug Administration added folic acid (the synthetic form of folate) to the list of vitamins and minerals that must be included in enriched grain foods. Unfortunately, as I've previously stated, most refined gluten-free grain foods are not enriched. However, with careful planning, you can still get the folic acid you need.

Folate is a generic term for one of the B vitamins. It is found in food in both natural and synthetic forms. When it occurs naturally in food (such as orange juice), it is generally referred to as folate. When a synthetic (manufactured) form of folate has been added to food or supplements, it is generally referred to as folic acid. Grain foods that are enriched or fortified, such as flour, bread, pasta, and breakfast cereal, contain synthetic folic acid.

The Dietary Reference Intake (DRI) for folate for adults is 400 micrograms of dietary folate equivalents. However, to help prevent neural-tube defects in their children, women who can become pregnant should consume 400 micrograms of synthetic folic acid from supplements or enriched foods in addition to the naturally occurring folate they get from food. The upper limit (maximum amount that should be consumed) for folic acid is 1,000 micrograms. No upper limit has been set for food folate.

It is important to understand that the various forms of folate are not created equal, and this is why you may see folate values given as dietary folate equivalents (DFE). This measure takes into consideration the differences in absorption between folate and folic acid. Food folate is less easily absorbed than the synthetic folic acid that is added to enriched foods and supplements. One microgram of food folate equals 1 DFE. A little over half of a microgram of synthetic folic acid equals 1 DFE.

Folate is necessary for enabling the cells in our body to divide, grow, and develop properly. The body needs enough folate to make red blood cells and to metabolize protein. During pregnancy, folate also ensures proper growth and development of the fetus.

The Gluten-Free Diet and Folate

With the proper food choices, a gluten-free diet can provide enough folate. However, it may be more difficult for a person following a gluten-free diet to consume recommended amounts of folic acid from enriched food than for a person following a more typical American diet. In the United States, most refined wheat-based flour, bread, pasta, and breakfast cereals are enriched or fortified with folic acid. However, because most refined gluten-free grain foods are not enriched, this source of folate is less readily available to people following a gluten-free diet.

Folate-Deficiency Anemia

Anemia can be defined as a decrease in the amount of hemoglobin in the blood. Hemoglobin is a protein found in red blood cells that carries oxygen to all the tissues of the body. Folate is required to make red blood cells, and without adequate amounts of folate because of poor dietary intake or poor absorption, red blood cells cannot develop properly. Folate-deficiency anemia is referred to as a macrocytic, megaloblastic anemia. This means there are low numbers of large, underdeveloped red blood cells that contain lower than normal amounts of hemoglobin. People with untreated celiac disease may not properly absorb folate or folic acid. When you are diagnosed with celiac disease, you should be assessed for both types of anemia: folate-deficiency anemia and iron-deficiency anemia.

Folate Deficiency and Cardiovascular Disease

According to the American Heart Association, high blood levels of the amino acid homocysteine are linked to an increased risk of coronary artery disease. There is some evidence to suggest that homocysteine traveling through the circulatory system may damage the walls of the arteries, leading to the development of fatty deposits. Folate is necessary to change the amino acid homocysteine into the amino acid methionine. If too little folate is available, blood levels of homocysteine will increase, so not getting enough folate in your gluten-free diet could put you at a greater risk for cardiovascular disease.

Adding Folate to Your Diet

You can increase your intake of folate by eating a variety of gluten-free foods. These include foods enriched with folic acid and foods that naturally contain folate.

Foods Enriched with Folic Acid. As previously discussed, eating foods that have been enriched with folic acid is very important if you are a female capable of becoming pregnant. Even if you do not fall into this category, folic acid from enriched foods or supplements (see Appendix A for a listing of manufacturers of gluten-free supplements) is more easily absorbed than folate from food. While most manufacturers of gluten-free flours, breads, pastas, and breakfast cereals do not enrich their products, a few do. Appendix C lists enriched gluten-free foods and their manufacturers. The following table gives the folic acid content of some enriched gluten-free foods available from several companies.

Gluten-Free Food Sources of Folic Acid		
Food	**Amount**	**Folic Acid**
ENJOY LIFE FOODS		
Bagels, Classic Original	1 bagel (91 grams)	140 micrograms
Bagels, Cinnamon Raisin	1 bagel (91 grams)	120 micrograms
Cereal, granola, Cinnamon Crunch	½ cup (52 grams)	140 micrograms
Cereal, granola, Very Berry Crunch	½ cup (52 grams)	100 micrograms
Cereal, granola, Cranapple Crunch	½ cup (52 grams)	80 micrograms
Snack bars, Caramel Apple	1 bar (28 grams)	140 micrograms
Snack bars, Cocoa Loco	1 bar (28 grams)	140 micrograms
Snack bars, Very Berry	1 bar (28 grams)	140 micrograms
ENER-G FOODS		
Bread, Raisin with Eggs	1 slice (39 grams)	32 micrograms
Bread, Hi-Fiber	1 slice (38 grams)	24 micrograms
Hamburger buns, Seattle Brown	1 bun (115 grams)	80 micrograms
Hot dog buns, Seattle Brown	1 bun (115 grams)	80 micrograms

Food	Amount	Folic Acid
PERKY'S NATURAL FOODS		
Cereal, Original Perky O's	¾ cup (33 grams)	180 micrograms
Cereal, Cinnamon Perky O's	¾ cup (33 grams)	120 micrograms
Cereal, Frosted Perky O's	¾ cup (33 grams)	120 micrograms
GENISOY		
Soy bars, Chunky Peanut Butter Fudge	1 bar (61.5 grams)	400 micrograms
Soy bars, Creamy Peanut Yogurt	1 bar (61.5 grams)	400 micrograms

Foods with Folate. Food sources of folate include legumes, green leafy vegetables, and fruit juices.

Folate Content of Selected Foods

Food	Amount	Dietary Folate Equivalent
Lentils (cooked)	½ cup	179 micrograms
Pinto beans (cooked)	½ cup	147 micrograms
Asparagus (cooked)	½ cup (6 spears)	134 micrograms
Spinach (cooked)	½ cup	131 micrograms
Black beans (cooked)	½ cup	128 micrograms
Navy beans (cooked)	½ cup	127 micrograms
Kidney beans (cooked)	½ cup	115 micrograms
Collards (cooked)	½ cup	88 micrograms
Turnip greens (cooked)	½ cup	85 micrograms
Broccoli (cooked)	½ cup	84 micrograms
Chick-peas (canned)	½ cup	80 micrograms
Orange juice (raw)	1 cup	74 micrograms
Split peas (cooked)	½ cup	64 micrograms
Tomato juice	1 cup	49 micrograms
Brussels sprouts (cooked)	½ cup (3–4 sprouts)	47 micrograms
Pineapple juice	1 cup	45 micrograms

All About Iron

At one point or another, many of us wonder if we're getting enough iron, especially if we're feeling tired or run-down. Perhaps you were diagnosed with iron-deficiency anemia before or at the same time as you were diagnosed with celiac disease. Fortunately, although some sources of iron may not be readily available to you on a gluten-free diet, iron abounds in many foods that are available.

Iron is a mineral that is found in food in two forms, heme iron and nonheme iron. Heme iron is found in animal products that contain muscle and blood, including beef, pork, poultry, and fish. Nonheme iron is found mostly in plant foods such as leafy green vegetables, dried fruits, and berries. Iron that is added to enriched foods is nonheme iron.

Iron is a necessary part of a protein called *hemoglobin*, which is found in red blood cells. The iron in hemoglobin attaches to oxygen and carries it through the bloodstream to all the tissues of the body. Iron also is a necessary part of a protein called *myo-globin*, which is found in muscle cells. As is the case with hemo-globin, the iron portion of myoglobin attaches to oxygen. This oxygen can be released and used by the muscle cells when muscles are active, as they are during exercise.

Science Class

In most people, the absorption of iron from food and supplements is well regulated by the body, which increases or decreases iron absorption depending on how much iron it needs. Some people, however, have a genetic condition called hemochromatosis, which causes iron to be absorbed regardless of the body's needs. These people may experience a buildup of iron (iron overload), which eventually can lead to tissue and organ damage. For more information on hemochromatosis, see the Centers for Disease Control and Prevention website at cdc.gov/ncbddd/hemochromatosis.

The Dietary Reference Intake (DRI) for iron for all adults except menstruating women is 8 milligrams per day. For menstruating women between the ages of nineteen and fifty, the DRI is 18 milligrams. The upper limit (the maximum amount that should be consumed) for iron is 45 milligrams.

The Gluten-Free Diet and Iron

With the proper food choices, a gluten-free diet can provide enough iron. However, a person following a gluten-free diet may find it more difficult to consume enough iron than a person following a typical American diet. This may be especially true for premenopausal women between the ages of nineteen and fifty, who require more than twice the amount of iron as similarly aged men. In the United States, grain-based foods account for a third of an adult's daily intake of iron, largely because of enrichment; most wheat-based grain foods are enriched with iron, and most mainstream breakfast cereals are fortified with iron. However, as mentioned, most refined gluten-free grain foods are not enriched, so this source of iron is not readily available to people with celiac disease. While whole grains also are an important source of iron, many gluten-free foods are made using refined flour and starch, so they contain very little iron.

Iron-Deficiency Anemia

As explained earlier, anemia can be defined as a decrease in the amount of hemoglobin in the blood. To make hemoglobin, the body needs iron. If the body doesn't have enough iron available to make hemoglobin, because of either poor dietary intake or poor absorption, iron-deficiency anemia may occur. Tiredness, one of the main symptoms of iron-deficiency anemia, is associated with the tissues of the body not getting enough oxygen. This type of anemia is referred to as a microcytic hypochromic anemia. This means that there are small red blood cells containing lower than normal amounts of hemoglobin.

Adding Iron to Your Diet

To increase your intake of iron, consume a variety of gluten-free whole and enriched grains, as well as lean meat, poultry, fish, legumes, vegetables, and fruits.

Whole-Grain or Enriched Gluten-Free Grain Foods. In the following table, various grain foods made from corn and rice are grouped together to show that whole grains and enriched grains contain more iron than refined, unenriched grains. Notice that teff and amaranth are iron superstars!

Iron Content of Selected Grain Foods		
Food	**Amount**	**Iron**
Teff flour	¼ cup	3.60 milligrams
Amaranth flour	¼ cup	2.70 milligrams
Buckwheat flour, whole-groat	¼ cup	1.22 milligrams
Wild rice, cooked	½ cup	0.49 milligrams
Corn flour, masa, enriched	¼ cup	2.05 milligrams
Popcorn, popped	1 ounce	0.90 milligram
Corn flour, whole-grain	¼ cup	0.70 milligram
Corn flour, degermed, unenriched	¼ cup	0.29 milligram
Cornstarch	¼ cup	0.15 milligram
White rice, enriched, cooked	½ cup	0.95 milligram
Brown-rice flour	¼ cup	0.78 milligram
Brown rice, cooked	½ cup	0.41 milligram
White rice, unenriched, cooked	½ cup	0.16 milligram
White-rice flour	¼ cup	0.14 milligram

Meat, Fish, and Beans. Beef, chicken, pork, fish, and eggs are sources of heme iron. Legumes, nuts, and seeds are sources of nonheme iron. According to *Dietary Guidelines for Americans, 2005,* if you require 2,000 calories each day, you should be eating five and a half *1-ounce equivalents* from this food group each day. A 1-ounce equivalent would be either 1 ounce of cooked beef, pork, chicken, and fish; one egg; ¼ cup of cooked dried beans, peas, or lentils; ¼ cup of tofu; 1 tablespoon of peanut butter; or ½ ounce of nuts or seeds.

If you like clams and oysters, you are in luck. They are iron superstars!

Iron Content of Foods from the Meat and Beans Group

Food	Amount	Iron
Clams (cooked)	1 ounce	7.93 milligrams
Oysters (cooked)	1 ounce	3.40 milligrams
Soybeans (cooked)	¼ cup	2.21 milligrams
Sesame seeds, whole	½ ounce (1½ tablespoons)	2.09 milligrams
White beans (cooked)	¼ cup	1.66 milligrams
Lentils (cooked)	¼ cup	1.65 milligrams
Tahini (ground sesame seeds)	1 tablespoon	1.34 milligrams
Kidney beans (cooked)	¼ cup	1.30 milligrams
Beef tenderloin, prime (cooked)	1 ounce	0.87 milligram
Scallops	1 ounce	0.85 milligram
Pine nuts	½ ounce (84 nuts)	0.78 milligram
Tofu (raw, firm)	1 ounce	0.75 milligram
Turkey, dark meat (with skin, cooked)	1 ounce	0.66 milligram
Almonds	½ ounce (11 nuts)	0.64 milligram
Split peas (cooked)	¼ cup	0.63 milligram
Egg (hard-boiled)	1 egg	0.59 milligram
Pumpkin seeds, whole	½ ounce (43 seeds)	0.47 milligram
Turkey breast (with skin, cooked)	1 ounce	0.45 milligram
Walnuts	½ ounce (7 halves)	0.41 milligram

continued

Iron Content of Foods from the Meat and Beans Group (continued)		
Food	**Amount**	**Iron**
Chicken drumstick (with skin, cooked)	1 ounce	0.38 milligram
Halibut	1 ounce	0.30 milligram
Peanut butter, chunky	1 tablespoon	0.30 milligram
Chicken breast (skin removed, cooked)	1 ounce	0.29 milligram
Salmon, wild	1 ounce	0.29 milligram
Pork chop (boneless, cooked)	1 ounce	0.22 milligram

Fruits and Vegetables. The fruits and vegetables in the following table are sources of nonheme iron.

Iron Content of Fruits and Vegetables		
Food	**Amount**	**Iron**
Spinach (cooked)	½ cup	3.21 milligrams
Pumpkin (canned)	½ cup	1.70 milligrams
Mushrooms (cooked)	½ cup	1.36 milligrams
Peas (cooked)	½ cup	1.22 milligrams
Collards (cooked)	½ cup	1.10 milligrams
Artichoke hearts (cooked)	½ cup	1.08 milligrams
Sauerkraut (canned)	½ cup	1.04 milligrams
Potato (baked, including skin)	½ medium	0.93 milligram
Raisins (seedless)	¼ cup	0.68 milligram
Beets (sliced, cooked)	½ cup	0.67 milligram
Sweet potato (baked)	½ large	0.62 milligram
Turnip greens (cooked)	½ cup	0.58 milligram

Iron Content of Fruits and Vegetables (continued)		
Food	**Amount**	**Iron**
Dates (chopped)	¼ cup	0.45 milligram
Raspberries (raw)	½ cup	0.42 milligram
Prunes	¼ cup	0.40 milligram
Strawberries (raw, sliced)	½ cup	0.34 milligram

Dark Chocolate. Yes, you read right. Each ounce of a dark-chocolate bar contains 0.60 milligram of iron. Look for bars with at least 60 percent cocoa content. Premium brands usually list the cocoa content on their label. Don't go overboard, though; this isn't license to gorge yourself on chocolate! Even dark chocolate is high in fat.

Increasing Your Absorption of Iron

Many factors affect the absorption of iron, both negatively and positively. Apply the following information to help you absorb as much iron as possible from the foods you eat:

❖ Heme iron (iron from animal foods) is better absorbed than nonheme iron (iron from plant foods, enriched foods, and supplements). This is opposite of the situation with folate, where food folate is less well absorbed than folic acid from supplements and enriched food.

❖ Antacids and calcium may decrease absorption of both heme and nonheme iron, because they lower the acidity of the stomach. For this reason, you may want to avoid taking antacids or calcium supplements with meals.

❖ Tea, coffee, and wine decrease absorption of nonheme iron. These drinks contain substances called tannins, which bind to iron and decrease its absorption.

❖ Vitamin C (or ascorbic acid) increases the absorption of nonheme iron. Vitamin C releases bound iron from substances such as tannins and changes it to a form that is more easily absorbed. For this reason, you should consider eating a source of vitamin C (containing at least 25 milligrams) with your meals.

Vitamin C Content of Selected Foods

Food	Serving Size	Vitamin C
Orange juice	1 cup	124.0 milligrams
Cranberry juice cocktail	1 cup	107.0 milligrams
Red pepper (raw)	½ cup chopped	95.1 milligrams
Grapefruit juice	1 cup	93.9 milligrams
Kiwifruit	½ cup (approximately 1 kiwi)	82.0 milligrams
Green pepper (raw)	½ cup chopped	59.9 milligrams
Broccoli (cooked)	½ cup chopped	50.6 milligrams
Strawberries	½ cup sliced	48.8 milligrams
Brussels sprouts (cooked)	½ cup	48.4 milligrams
Orange segments	½ cup (approximately 1 small orange)	41.6 milligrams

All About Thiamin, Riboflavin, and Niacin

Most people don't worry much about their intake of thiamin, riboflavin, and niacin; these nutrients aren't big news makers. This is because refined grain foods have been enriched with them for so long that deficiencies of these vitamins are no longer viewed as an issue. Deficiencies of these vitamins are rare in the United States, largely because of the widespread enrichment and fortification of wheat-based flours, breads, pasta, and breakfast cereals. However, these nutrients are important for you to think about, because most refined gluten-free grain foods are not enriched.

Historical Nugget

Government recommendations to enrich flour and bread products with the B vitamins thiamin, riboflavin, and niacin (as well as iron) were first made in the early 1940s. These recommendations came about because of the poor nutritional status of enlisted men during World War II, as well as the identification of specific vitamin-deficiency diseases related to poor dietary intake of B vitamins. Deficiency diseases such as pellagra (due to poor niacin intake) and beriberi (due to poor thiamin intake) are rarely seen in the United States today, largely eliminated by enrichment of cereal grains.

Thiamin, riboflavin, and niacin are B vitamins, also known as vitamin B_1 (thiamin), vitamin B_2 (riboflavin), and vitamin B_3 (niacin). The body requires B vitamins for the proper metabolism of food and the production of energy. The Dietary Reference Intakes (DRIs) for thiamin, riboflavin, and niacin differ for men and women:

Vitamin	Adult Males	Adult Females
Thiamin	1.2 milligrams/day	1.1 milligrams/day
Riboflavin	1.3 milligrams/day	1.1 milligrams/day
Niacin	16 milligrams/day	14 milligrams/day

The Gluten-Free Diet and Thiamin, Riboflavin, and Niacin

With proper meal planning, a gluten-free diet can provide enough thiamin, riboflavin, and niacin. However, a person following a gluten-free diet may find it harder to consume enough of these vitamins than would someone following a typical American diet.

In the United States, grain-based foods account for approximately 30 percent of an adult's daily intake of thiamin, riboflavin, and niacin, largely because of the enrichment of these foods with B vitamins. In contrast, as stated in the sections on iron and folate, most gluten-free breads, pastas, and breakfast cereals are not enriched or fortified.

Adding Thiamin, Riboflavin, and Niacin to Your Diet

The following suggestions should help you increase your intake of thiamin, riboflavin, and niacin:

❖ **Choose whole-grain gluten-free products over refined gluten-free products whenever possible.** Examples of gluten-free whole grains include amaranth, brown rice, buckwheat, millet, quinoa, sorghum, teff, wild rice, whole cornmeal, and whole corn flour. Appendix C lists gluten-free whole grains and their manufacturers.

❖ **Choose enriched gluten-free grain foods over refined, unenriched varieties whenever possible.** While most manufacturers of specially formulated gluten-free flours, breads, pastas, and breakfast cereals do not enrich their products, an increasing number do. Appendix C lists enriched gluten-free foods and their manufacturers.

❖ **Consume nongrain sources of these nutrients.** The following tables suggest sources of each nutrient.

Thiamin Content of Selected Foods		
Food	**Amount**	**Thiamin Content**
Pork chop (broiled)	3 ounces	0.55 milligram
Trout (cooked)	3 ounces	0.36 milligram
Pistachios	1 ounce (49 nuts)	0.24 milligram
Salmon (cooked)	3 ounces	0.23 milligram
Orange juice	1 cup	0.22 milligram

Food	Amount	Thiamin Content
Black beans (cooked)	½ cup	0.21 milligram
Green peas (cooked)	½ cup	0.21 milligram
Split peas (cooked)	½ cup	0.19 milligram
Brazil nuts	1 ounce (6 nuts)	0.18 milligram
Lentils (cooked)	½ cup	0.17 milligram
Soy milk	1 cup	0.15 milligram

Riboflavin Content of Selected Foods

Food	Amount	Riboflavin Content
Cottage cheese, low-fat	2 cups	0.75 milligram
Yogurt, plain, low-fat	1 cup	0.52 milligram
Milk, low-fat	1 cup	0.45 milligram
Pork chop (broiled)	3 ounces	0.25 milligram
Soybeans (cooked)	½ cup	0.25 milligram
Almonds	1 ounce (22 nuts)	0.24 milligram
Mushrooms (cooked)	½ cup	0.23 milligram
Spinach (cooked)	½ cup	0.21 milligram

Niacin Content of Selected Foods

Food	Amount	Niacin Content
Tuna (fresh, cooked)	3 ounces	10.1 milligrams
Swordfish (cooked)	3 ounces	10.0 milligrams
Salmon (cooked)	3 ounces	8.6 milligrams
Halibut (cooked)	3 ounces	6.1 milligrams
Turkey breast (cooked)	3 ounces	5.9 milligrams
Peanuts	1 ounce (28 nuts)	3.8 milligrams
Pork chop (broiled)	3 ounces	3.5 milligrams
Sunflower seeds	1 ounce (approximately ¼ cup)	2.0 milligrams
Lentils (cooked)	½ cup	1.0 milligram

All About Dietary Fat and Cholesterol

We need some fat in our diets to be healthy. We just don't need a lot of it. When we follow a gluten-free diet, the nutritional composition of our diet may change. Unfortunately, if we consume fewer carbohydrates because many familiar grain foods are off limits, we may increase our fat intake by adding fatty foods to replace the foods we can no longer eat. However, awareness of this pitfall can help you avoid it. The information in this section will help you limit your fat intake as well as choose the right kind of fat.

Dietary fat is the most concentrated source of food energy, providing more than twice the number of calories per gram as carbohydrate or protein. One gram of fat contains 9 calories, while each gram of carbohydrate or protein contains 4 calories. Fat provides you with essential fatty acids and helps your body absorb the fat-soluble vitamins (vitamins A, D, E, and K).

Fats are found in both animal and plant foods. They are classified as saturated, polyunsaturated, or monounsaturated, depending on the major fatty acid they contain. These various types of fatty acids have different chemical structures and therefore different effects on the body. Saturated fatty acids are the major fatty acids in animal fats (meat, poultry, milk, eggs) and tropical oils (palm, palm kernel, coconut). Saturated fats are generally solid at room temperature. Polyunsaturated and monounsaturated fats are found in vegetable oils such as canola, peanut, olive, safflower, sunflower, corn, and soybean. They also are the main fats in fish, nuts, seeds, olives, and avocados. Polyunsaturated and monounsaturated fats tend to be liquid at room temperature.

Another type of fat is trans fat or trans-fatty acids. While some trans fat occurs naturally in food, it is primarily a manufactured fat, created when hydrogen is added to liquid fat (such as vegetable oil) to make solid fat (such as margarine). The addition of hydrogen to liquid fats is called hydrogenation. Manufacturers use hydrogenated fats in products to increase their shelf life. Trans fat is found in any food whose ingredients include partially hydrogenated vegetable oil; such foods may include margarine, vegetable shortening, and snack foods (crackers, cookies, potato chips). Since January 1, 2006, the Food and Drug Administration has required that trans fat be included on the Nutrition Facts label.

Science Class

On some processed food products, the Nutrition Facts label lists the trans fat content as 0, even though the list of ingredients includes hydrogenated oil. How can this apparently contradictory information be true? Under FDA regulations, a manufacturer may state on the label that a product contains 0 grams of trans fat as long as the product contains less than 0.5 gram of trans fat per product serving.

Dietary Guidelines for Americans, 2005 recommends that fat intake be kept at 20 to 35 percent of calories. Less than 10 percent of calories should come from saturated fat, and intake of trans fat should be kept as low as possible. The American Heart Association has slightly stricter recommendations, suggesting that saturated-fat intake should be less than 7 percent of calories, and trans fat less than 1 percent of calories.

The Gluten-Free Diet and Fat

There is nothing inherent in a gluten-free diet that makes it more (or less) likely to be high in fat. Nonetheless, studies on the nutritional composition of gluten-free diets have found fat intake to be higher than recommendations. The reasons for this are multifaceted and include below-recommended intake of grain foods.

In fact, some studies have reported that when gluten-containing grain foods are removed from the diet, people tend to replace them with high-fat foods instead of gluten-free grain foods.

For overall health and well-being, people with celiac disease should make sure they are consuming recommended amounts of grain foods and pay attention to the fat content of their diet, especially as it concerns saturated and trans fat. Any diet that contains full-fat dairy products, processed snack foods, and fatty meat products may be high in unhealthful fat.

In addition, while a high-fat diet doesn't necessarily translate to excess body fat, it certainly increases the likelihood that this will occur. Many people with celiac disease find that, as their intestine heals and they are better able to absorb nutrients from the food they eat, they gain weight, sometimes more than they desire. One of the easiest ways to prevent this from happening (or to lose weight if desired) is to lower the amount of total fat in the diet.

Why You Should Be Aware of the Type of Fat in Your Diet

Saturated fat and trans fat increase the LDL (bad) cholesterol in your blood. High levels of LDL cholesterol are associated with an increased risk of developing heart disease. This type of cholesterol may accumulate on artery walls and over time may decrease the amount of space for blood to flow. If a blockage occurs and not enough oxygen-rich blood is able to get to the heart, a heart attack may occur. Monounsaturated and polyunsaturated fat, when used in place of (not in addition to) saturated fat, tend to be associated with lower levels of LDL cholesterol.

Why You Need Essential Fatty Acids

Polyunsaturated fats contain essential fatty acids (fatty acids that are necessary for good health and are not produced by the body).

Omega-3 fatty acids—eicosapentaenoic acid (EPA) and docosahexaenoic acid (DHA), found in fish, especially wild salmon, lake trout, and canned light tuna*—are one category of essential fatty acids. Omega-3 fatty acids may reduce the risk of heart disease by reducing the risk of blood clot formation. The American Heart Association recommends that you eat fish, especially oily fish, at least twice a week. The association also recommends that you consume sources of alpha-linolenic acid (LNA), which can be converted to EPA and DHA in the body. Sources of LNA include flaxseed, which conveniently is frequently added to processed gluten-free foods. Other sources are walnuts and canola oil. For more information on omega-3 fatty acids, see the American Heart Association's website, americanheart.org.

Cholesterol

Cholesterol is a fatlike substance that is found in every cell of the human body and is required for several physiological processes. The body is able to manufacture all the cholesterol it requires, so there is no reason to consume it from food sources. Furthermore, like saturated fat and trans fat, dietary cholesterol increases the LDL cholesterol in your blood, thereby increasing your risk of developing heart disease.

Cholesterol is found only in animal products, such as meat, fish, poultry, milk products, and eggs. It is not found in plant foods, such as fruits, vegetables, grains, and legumes.

According to the *Dietary Guidelines for Americans, 2005*, your cholesterol intake should be less than 300 milligrams a day. This is also the recommendation of the American Heart Association.

---

*Canned *white* meat tuna (for example, albacore) contains higher amounts of omega-3 fatty acids than canned light meat tuna, but it also contains higher levels of mercury. For this reason, choose *light* tuna over white tuna.

Eating Less Total Fat, Saturated Fat, Trans Fat, and Cholesterol

The following guidelines should help you decrease the amount of total fat, saturated fat, trans fat, and cholesterol in your diet:

❖ **Eat generous amounts of fruits, vegetables, and whole grains.** In general, these foods contain very little, if any, fat.

❖ **Choose beans, fish, nuts, and seeds as your protein foods most of the time.** These foods contain mostly polyunsaturated and monounsaturated fat. Fish that is fresh, plain frozen, or water packed is best. Wild salmon and lake trout contain healthful omega-3 fatty acids. Nuts and seeds that are raw or dry roasted (meaning without added oil) are best. Because of the fat content of nuts and seeds, you should limit your intake of these foods to ¼ cup per day. With the exception of soybeans (which contain healthful unsaturated fat), beans are low in fat.

❖ **Choose lean cuts of red meat.** Lean cuts of beef include select-grade top round, top loin, eye of round, sirloin, and tenderloin. Lean cuts of pork include trimmed tenderloin, loin roast, center loin chop, and top loin chop. To further reduce your fat consumption, trim the fat off red meat before cooking it.

❖ **Choose skinless, white-meat poultry.** Poultry products with skin are higher in fat than products with the skin removed. Also, dark-meat poultry, such as a chicken leg or thigh, is higher in fat than white-meat poultry, such as a chicken breast or wing.

❖ **Limit consumption of high-fat protein foods.** Bacon, sausage, bologna, and salami have high fat content. Think of these foods more as "special occasion" foods or side dishes to be used very sparingly.

❖ **Limit consumption of regular hamburger.** Use ground beef that is at least 90 percent lean. When using higher-fat hamburger, drain off the extra fat after cooking, or use a cooking method, such as grilling, that allows the fat to drip away from the meat.

❖ **Eat low-fat or nonfat milk products.** Choose skim or 1 percent milk, low-fat yogurt, and low-fat cheese. If you eat a lot of full-fat milk products, this one change alone will dramatically decrease your intake of total fat and saturated fat.

❖ **Limit consumption of processed foods high in total fat, saturated fat, or trans fat.** Always check the Nutrition Facts label and ingredient list for trans fat. If a product contains this type of fat, do not buy it. Instead, find a comparable product made without trans fat. Also, some gluten-free snack foods are very high in fat. Always check labels, and choose products with lower fat content.

❖ **Prepare as much food at home as possible.** By preparing your own food, you control the amount and type of fat you eat. You are less likely to unknowingly consume saturated and trans fat.

❖ **Limit the amount of butter and margarine you use.** If a recipe gives you the choice of using butter or oil, always use oil. When you sauté vegetables, use vegetable oil, not butter. Besides limiting butter and margarine in cooking, find substitutes at the table. For example, dip bread in olive oil instead of spreading it with butter. One tablespoon of olive oil contains 13.5 grams of total fat, 1.9 grams of saturated fat, and no cholesterol. In comparison, 1 tablespoon of butter contains 11.5 grams of total fat, 7.3 grams of saturated fat, and 31 milligrams of cholesterol.

As you can see from the comparisons in the following table, choosing lower-fat versions of foods can make a major difference in your overall intake of fat and saturated fat.

Comparisons of Fat and Saturated-Fat Content

Milk (1 cup)

Type	Total Fat	Saturated Fat
Whole milk	8.0 grams	4.5 grams
2 percent milk	5.0 grams	3.0 grams
1 percent milk	2.5 grams	1.5 grams
Skim milk	0.0 grams	0.0 grams

YOGURT, PLAIN (1 CUP)

Type	Total Fat	Saturated Fat
Whole-milk yogurt	8.0 grams	5.0 grams
Low-fat yogurt	4.0 grams	2.5 grams
Fat-free yogurt	0.5 gram	0.5 gram

CHEDDAR CHEESE (1 OUNCE)

Type	Total Fat	Saturated Fat
Whole-milk cheese	9.5 grams	6.0 grams
Low-fat cheese	2.0 grams	1.0 gram

POULTRY (3 OUNCES)

Type	Total Fat	Saturated Fat
Chicken leg (with skin)	11.5 grams	3.0 grams
Chicken leg (without skin)	7.0 grams	2.0 grams
Chicken breast (with skin)	6.5 grams	2.0 grams
Chicken breast (without skin)	3.0 grams	1.0 gram

BEEF (3 OUNCES)

Type	Total Fat	Saturated Fat
95 percent lean hamburger	5.5 grams	2.5 grams
90 percent lean hamburger	10.0 grams	4.0 grams
85 percent lean hamburger	13.0 grams	5.0 grams
80 percent lean hamburger	15.0 grams	6.0 grams

COOKIE (1 COOKIE, 23 G)

Type	Total Fat	Saturated Fat
Pamela's pecan shortbread	8.0 grams	4.0 grams
Pamela's ginger	5.0 grams	0.5 gram

Weight Loss and Dieting

If you have gained some unwanted weight since being diagnosed with celiac disease, dieting may seem like a logical option, but it probably is not the answer.

Weight loss in America is big business. As a country, we spend billions of dollars trying to lose weight. While many individuals succeed at shedding pounds, only a very small percentage of those who lose weight through dieting are able to maintain their weight loss. Many of those who regain the pounds make further attempts to lose weight. This yo-yo dieting, as it is called, may contribute to several health problems.

Yo-yo dieting may result in a higher risk of heart disease and diabetes. When fat is regained after dieting, it may be stored around the abdomen. Abdominal fat storage, in contrast to fat stored in the leg or hip region, appears to be a risk factor in the development of certain diseases. Yo-yo dieting also may increase your percent of body fat. When you lose weight through dieting, you lose both fat and muscle tissue. However, when you stop dieting, excess calories are stored in the form of fat. Therefore, even if you regain only as many pounds as you lost through dieting, your body is likely to be fattier than it was previously.

Also, when your percent of body fat increases, your metabolic rate (the rate at which your body burns calories) declines. This happens because muscle tissue is more metabolically active than fat. Hence, if your percent of body fat increases after regaining lost weight, your body will not be able to burn as many calories.

It is important to keep in mind that diets are for the purpose of weight loss, not weight maintenance. All too often, when a diet is completed, the former dieter goes back to the same eating habits that caused him or her to gain weight in the first place. So instead of struggling with a weight-loss regime, do yourself a favor, and focus on making positive, permanent changes in your eating habits by following the guidelines outlined in the next chapter of this book.

5

Ensuring a Nutritious Gluten-Free Diet

[We] believe the moment has come to devote more attention to problems regarding correct follow-up of [celiac disease], not only the compliance with diet, but also nutritional balance of the diet itself.

—Paolo Mariani, Italian researcher, 1998

TO IMPROVE THE quality of your diet, you first need to know what you should be eating. The tips in this chapter are based on the *Dietary Guidelines for Americans*, updated every five years by the U.S. Department of Health and Human Services and Department of Agriculture. To find out more, go to the Dietary Guidelines website of the Department of Health and Human Services, healthierus.gov/dietaryguidelines.

THE KEYS TO A HEALTHFUL DIET

❖ Eat a variety of nutrient-dense foods and beverages each day. A nutrient-dense food is one that provides a large amount of a nutrient or nutrients for the calorie content of the food. For example, a 100-calorie serving of banana is more nutrient dense than 100 calories of soda.

❖ Limit intake of foods containing saturated fat, trans fat, cholesterol, added sugar, and added salt.

- ✤ Eat a variety of fruits and vegetables each day. A person requiring 2,000 calories a day should consume 2 cups of fruit and 2½ cups of vegetables daily.
- ✤ Eat whole grains. At least half of your grain servings should be whole grains. The remainder of your grain servings should come from either whole-grain or enriched products. A person requiring 2,000 calories a day should consume six 1-ounce-equivalent servings of grains, and at least three of the servings should be whole grains.
- ✤ Drink 3 cups of nonfat or low-fat milk (or consume the equivalent) each day.

Historical Nugget

Dietary Guidelines for Americans, first published in 1980, differs greatly from early food guides. The guide shown here was developed by the U.S. Department of Agriculture and the Food and Drug Administration sometime before 1940.

Source: U.S. Department of Agriculture, Food and Nutrition Information Center, "Early Food Guides (1894–1940)," *Historical Food Guides Background and Development,* last modified September 2002, nal.usda .gov/fnic/history/early.htm.

U. S. DEPT. OF AGRICULTURE   U.S. FOOD ADMINISTRATION

Choose Your Food Wisely

STUDY THESE FIVE FOOD GROUPS

Every food you eat may be put into one of these groups. Each group serves a special purpose in nourishing your body. You should choose some food from each group daily.

1. VEGETABLES AND FRUITS.
2. MILK, EGGS, FISH, MEAT, CHEESE, BEANS, PEAS, PEANUTS.
3. CEREALS—CORN MEAL, OATMEAL, RICE, BREAD, ETC.
4. SUGAR, SIRUPS, JELLY, HONEY, ETC.
5. FATS—BUTTER, MARGARINE, COTTONSEED OIL, OLIVE OIL, DRIPPINGS, SUET.

You can exchange one food for another *in the same group.* For example, oatmeal may be used instead of wheat, and eggs, or sometimes beans, instead of meat; but oatmeal can not be used instead of milk. Use both oatmeal and milk.

YOU NEED SOME FOOD FROM EACH GROUP EVERY DAY—DON'T SKIP ANY

What to Eat Every Day

Based on recommendations developed by the U.S. Department of Agriculture, the following tables give you an idea of how much from each food group you should be eating each day. Choose the profile that most closely resembles you, or for a more accurate amount based on your weight, height, and age, check out the USDA's MyPyramid website, mypyramid.gov.

To use the following tables, first determine your approximate calorie needs. Then, based on the number of calories you should consume, determine the amounts from each food group that you should be eating.

Calorie Needs			
Males	**Sedentary***	**Moderately Active***	**Active***
Age 19–20	2,600	2,800	3,000
Age 21–25	2,400	2,800	3,000
Age 26–30	2,400	2,600	3,000
Age 31–35	2,400	2,600	3,000
Age 36–40	2,400	2,600	2,800
Age 41–45	2,200	2,600	2,800
Age 46–50	2,200	2,400	2,800
Age 51–55	2,200	2,400	2,800
Age 56–60	2,200	2,400	2,600
Age 61–65	2,000	2,400	2,600
Age 66–70	2,000	2,200	2,600
Age 71–75	2,000	2,200	2,600
Age 76 and older	2,000	2,200	2,400
Females	**Sedentary***	**Moderately Active***	**Active***
Age 19–20	2,000	2,200	2,400
Age 21–25	2,000	2,200	2,400

continued

Calorie Needs (continued)

Females	Sedentary*	Moderately Active*	Active*
Age 26–30	1,800	2,000	2,400
Age 31–35	1,800	2,000	2,200
Age 36–40	1,800	2,000	2,200
Age 41–45	1,800	2,000	2,200
Age 46–50	1,800	2,000	2,200
Age 51–55	1,600	1,800	2,200
Age 56–60	1,600	1,800	2,200
Age 61–65	1,600	1,800	2,000
Age 66–70	1,600	1,800	2,000
Age 71–75	1,600	1,800	2,000
Age 76 and over	1,600	1,800	2,000

*Sedentary means you get less than 30 minutes a day of moderate physical activity in addition to daily activities. Moderately active means you get 30 to 60 minutes a day of moderate physical activity in addition to daily activities. Active means you get 60 or more minutes a day of moderate physical activity in addition to daily activities.

Source: U.S. Department of Agriculture, Center for Nutrition Policy and Promotion, April 2005.

Daily Amount of Food from Each Group

Food Group	Calorie Level							
	1,600	1,800	2,000	2,200	2,400	2,600	2,800	3,000
Fruits (cups)	1½	1½	2	2	2	2	2½	2½
Vegetables (cups) (cups)	2	2½	2½	3	3	3½	3½	4
Grains (ounce-equivalents)	5	6	6	7	8	9	10	10
Meat and beans (ounce-equivalents)	5	5	5½	6	6½	6½	7	7
Milk (cups)	3	3	3	3	3	3	3	3
Oils (teaspoons)	5	5	6	6	7	8	8	11

Source: U.S. Department of Agriculture, Center for Nutrition Policy and Promotion, April 2005.

What You Eat Now: Food Records

Now that you know how much you should be eating, the second step to improving the quality of your diet is to develop a record of what you actually are eating. A food record is a great tool for improving your diet. When you keep a food record, you literally record everything you eat and drink for a predetermined amount of time. Having this type of visual aid will help you see what foods you need to eat more or less of.

Keeping a Food Record

To get the most information out of your food record, follow these guidelines:

* Take three sheets of paper and label them "Day 1," "Day 2," and "Day 3." On each sheet make three columns and label them "Food/Beverage," "Description," and "Amount."
* Choose a three-day period of time when your eating habits are likely to represent your typical habits. For example, you probably would not want to include a holiday in your recording period.
* Record everything you eat and drink over this three-day period. No one is going to see this record but you, so include *everything*.

Personal Viewpoint

Please don't skip this exercise because you think it will be too inconvenient or believe you can remember everything you eat. Having a written record of everything you eat really is the only way for you to actually see the amounts and types of food you are providing your body. Until you really know what you are eating, it is impossible to make any improvements.

❖ Record this information as soon as possible after eating and as completely and accurately as possible.

❖ Provide a complete description of each food and beverage, including brand names. Keep the labels with nutritional information and ingredients so you can refer back to them when completing your worksheets.

❖ Record the amount consumed of each food and beverage. For cooked foods, record the amount of cooked product consumed, using household measures (for example, ½ cup cooked brown rice or noodles), or approximate the size (one medium-size baked potato). For foods that can be counted, approximate the size of the food and the amount eaten (one medium-size apple, three small cookies). Use the unit of measure that is common for the type of product consumed: tablespoons for peanut butter; cups for dry cereal, pasta, and rice; ounces for beverages and cheese.

❖ Record the amount and type of any fat, including oil, butter, margarine, mayonnaise, and salad dressing, used in cooking and added at the table. Record the amount in teaspoons (3 teaspoons equals 1 tablespoon).

❖ If the food is homemade, save the recipe, and record the percentage of the recipe that you ate.

❖ If the food is a commercial mix or ready-made gluten-free product, keep the label so you can refer back to it when completing your worksheets.

❖ If you are eating in a restaurant, provide a complete description of the meal, and record the amount of each food eaten.

Remember, the more accurate the information you include in your food record, the more accurate your assessment of your eating habits will be.

Assessing Your Food Record: Worksheets

Using the information you created in your food records as well as the food labels you saved, complete the following worksheets. These categorize the amounts you ate as grains, vegetables, fruits, milk, meat and beans, and oils.

Worksheet 1: Grains

How many ounce-equivalents of grains did you eat each day? In general, count each of the following amounts as 1 ounce:

- ❖ Amaranth, cooked, ½ cup
- ❖ Bread, 1 slice
- ❖ Buckwheat, cooked, ½ cup
- ❖ Cereal, cooked, ½ cup
- ❖ Cereal, 1 cup ready-to-eat
- ❖ Millet, cooked, ½ cup
- ❖ Oatmeal (gluten-free), cooked, ½ cup
- ❖ Pasta, cooked, ½ cup
- ❖ Popcorn, 3 cups popped
- ❖ Quinoa, cooked, ½ cup
- ❖ Rice, cooked, ½ cup
- ❖ Sorghum, cooked, ½ cup
- ❖ Teff, cooked, ½ cup
- ❖ Tortilla (corn), 1
- ❖ Wild rice, cooked, ½ cup

For crackers, muffins, rice cakes, pancakes, waffles, and other grain foods, check the Nutrition Facts label. The serving size will be listed in grams. One ounce is approximately equal to 28 grams. So, for example, if you ate three rice cakes, and each rice cake weighed 9 grams, you would have consumed about 1 ounce of rice cakes. For more information about what counts as an ounce of grain food, visit the MyPyramid nutrition website, mypyramid.gov.

Day	Amount Eaten: Grain Foods
Day 1	_____ ounces
Day 2	_____ ounces
Day 3	_____ ounces
Total three-day intake	_____ ounces
Average daily intake	_____ ounces (total intake divided by 3)
Recommended intake	_____ ounces (from table earlier in this chapter)

Compare your average daily intake to the recommended intake. How much more (or less) grain food should you be eating?

_____ ounces of grain foods

How many ounces of your grain foods were whole grains? (Gluten-free whole grains include whole cornmeal, whole corn flour, popcorn, brown rice, brown-rice flour, wild rice, oatmeal, buckwheat groats, buckwheat flour, amaranth, amaranth flour, millet meal, millet flour, quinoa, quinoa flour, sorghum, sorghum flour, teff, teff flour.)

_____ ounces of whole grains

Remember, at least half of the grain foods you eat should be whole grains.

How many ounces of your grain foods were enriched with B vitamins and iron? (If a product includes added vitamins and minerals, these will be included within the ingredient list, or there will be a separate listing following the ingredient list.)

_____ ounces of enriched grains

Remember, grain foods you consume that are not whole grain should be enriched.

Worksheet 2: Vegetables

How many cups of vegetables did you eat each day? In general, count each of the following as 1 cup:

* Raw vegetables, 1 cup
* Cooked vegetables, 1 cup
* Vegetable juice, 1 cup
* Leafy greens, 2 cups
* Beans, cooked, 1 cup (for example, kidney, black, or garbanzo beans)
* Bell pepper (green), 1 large
* Bell pepper (red), 1 large
* Broccoli, 3 spears
* Carrots, 2 medium
* Celery, 2 large stalks
* Corn, 1 ear
* Potato, baked or boiled, 1 medium
* Sweet potato, baked, 1 large
* Tofu, 1 cup
* Tomato, 1 large

For more information on what counts as a cup of vegetables, go to mypyramid.gov.

Day	Amount Eaten: Vegetables
Day 1	_____ cups
Day 2	_____ cups
Day 3	_____ cups
Total three-day intake	_____ cups

Average daily intake _____ cups (total intake
divided by 3)

Recommended intake _____ cups (from table earlier
in this chapter)

Compare your average daily intake to the recommended intake. How many more (or fewer) cups of vegetables should you be eating?
_____ cups of vegetables

Worksheet 3: Fruits

How many cups of fruit did you eat each day? In general, count each of the following as 1 cup:

- ❖ Fruit, 1 cup
- ❖ Fruit juice, 100 percent, 1 cup
- ❖ Dried fruit (for example, raisins, apricots, apples), ½ cup
- ❖ Apple, ½ large
- ❖ Apple, 1 small
- ❖ Applesauce, 1 cup
- ❖ Banana, 1 large
- ❖ Grapes, 32
- ❖ Grapefruit, 1 medium
- ❖ Orange, 1 large
- ❖ Peach, 1 large
- ❖ Pear, 1 medium
- ❖ Plums, 3 medium
- ❖ Plums, 2 large
- ❖ Strawberries, 8 large
- ❖ Watermelon, 1 small wedge

For more information on what counts as a cup of fruit, go to mypyramid.gov.

Day	Amount Eaten: Fruits
Day 1	_____ cups
Day 2	_____ cups
Day 3	_____ cups
Total three-day intake	_____ cups
Average daily intake	_____ cups (total intake divided by 3)
Recommended intake	_____ cups (from table earlier in this chapter)

Compare your average daily intake to the recommended intake. How many more (or fewer) cups of fruit should you be eating?

_____ cups of fruit

Worksheet 4: Milk and Milk Alternatives

How many cups of milk (or the equivalent) did you consume each day? In general, count each of the following as 1 cup:

* Milk (regular or lactose-free), 1 cup
* Yogurt, 1 cup
* Cheese, natural, 1½ ounces
* Cheese, processed, 2 ounces
* Cheese, ⅓ cup shredded
* Cottage cheese, 2 cups
* Ricotta cheese, ½ cup
* Frozen yogurt, 1 cup
* Ice cream, 1½ cups
* Pudding, 1 cup

For more information on what counts as 1 cup of milk, go to mypyramid.gov.

If you do not consume dairy products, count the following nondairy products as 1 cup milk (these calcium-fortified products contain about 300 milligrams of calcium, which is approximately the amount of calcium found in 1 cup of milk).

❖ 1 cup calcium-fortified orange juice
❖ 1 cup calcium-fortified soy milk
❖ ½ block tofu prepared with calcium sulfate

Note: The calcium content of calcium-prepared tofu varies greatly. Check the Nutrition Facts label of the particular brand of tofu you ate. This label will indicate the percentage of the Daily Value for calcium. To determine the amount of calcium, multiply this percentage by 1,000 milligrams (the Daily Value for calcium). To multiply the percentage, first convert it to a decimal. For example 30 percent calcium becomes 0.30. Multiplied by 1,000 milligrams, you get 300 milligrams. Every 300 milligrams you consumed counts as 1 cup of milk, and every 150 milligrams you consumed counts as ½ cup of milk.

Day	Amount Eaten: Milk and Milk Alternatives
Day 1	_____ cups
Day 2	_____ cups
Day 3	_____ cups
Total three-day intake	_____ cups
Average daily intake	_____ cups (total intake divided by 3)
Recommended intake	_____ cups (from table earlier in this chapter)

Compare your average daily intake to the recommended intake. How much more (or less) milk and milk alternatives should you be consuming?
_____ cups

How many cups of milk (or the equivalent) were low-fat or nonfat?

_____ cups

Remember, the milk products you consume should be low-fat or nonfat.

If you do not drink milk or consume other foods fortified with calcium, it is important to consume other food sources of calcium. To identify nondairy sources of calcium, see Chapter 4.

Worksheet 5: Meat and Beans

How many ounces of meat and beans (or the equivalent) did you eat each day? In general, count each of the following as 1 ounce from the meat and beans group:

- ❖ Beef, cooked, 1 ounce
- ❖ Pork or ham, cooked, 1 ounce
- ❖ Chicken or turkey, cooked, 1 ounce
- ❖ Deli meat, 1 ounce
- ❖ Fish, 1 ounce
- ❖ Shellfish, 1 ounce
- ❖ Egg, 1
- ❖ Beans (for example, kidney, black, pinto), cooked, ¼ cup
- ❖ Baked beans, ¼ cup
- ❖ Hummus, 2 tablespoons
- ❖ Refried beans, ¼ cup
- ❖ Legume-based soup (for example, split pea or lentil), gluten-free, ½ cup
- ❖ Veggie burger, gluten-free, soy-based, ½
- ❖ Nuts, ½ ounce
- ❖ Nut butter (almond, cashew, soy), 1 tablespoon
- ❖ Peanut butter, 1 tablespoon
- ❖ Seeds, ½ ounce
- ❖ Tempeh, cooked, 1 ounce
- ❖ Tofu, ¼ cup (approximately 2 ounces)

For more information about what counts as a 1-ounce-equivalent from the meat and beans group, go to mypyramid.gov.

Day	Amount Eaten: Meat and Beans
Day 1	_____ ounces
Day 2	_____ ounces
Day 3	_____ ounces
Total three-day intake	_____ ounces
Average daily intake	_____ ounces (total intake divided by 3)
Recommended intake	_____ ounces (from table earlier in this chapter)

Compare your average daily intake to the recommended intake. How many more or fewer 1-ounce-equivalents from the meat and beans group should you be eating?

_____ 1-ounce-equivalents of meat and beans

How many of your ounces were fish, beans, nuts, seeds, tofu, lean or low-fat meat, poultry without the skin, or low-fat deli meat (for example, sliced turkey breast)?

_____ ounces

Remember to choose meats and equivalents that minimize unhealthful fats:

* ❖ Choose lean cuts of beef and pork.
* ❖ Choose hamburger that is at least 90 percent fat free.
* ❖ Purchase skinless poultry, or remove the skin before cooking (unless you are preparing whole poultry products).
* ❖ When choosing deli meats, choose lower-fat products such as turkey breast instead of higher-fat products like bologna and salami.
* ❖ Eat fish at least twice a week. The fat in fish is primarily polyunsaturated and monounsaturated.

❖ Get some of your meat equivalents from beans. Beans are generally low in fat.

❖ Include small servings of nuts and seeds, which provide healthful fatty acids. The fat in nuts and seeds is primarily polyunsaturated and monounsaturated.

Worksheet 6: Oils

How many teaspoons of oil did you eat each day? Use the following equivalents to help you determine your oil intake:

❖ 1 tablespoon vegetable oil = 3 teaspoons oil
❖ 1 tablespoon margarine (with no trans fat) = 2½ teaspoons oil
❖ 1 tablespoon mayonnaise = 2½ teaspoons oil
❖ 2 tablespoons salad dressing = 2 teaspoons oil
❖ 8 large olives = 1 teaspoon oil
❖ ½ medium avocado = 3 teaspoons oil
❖ 2 tablespoons peanut butter = 4 teaspoons oil
❖ 1 ounce nuts or seeds = 3 teaspoons oil

For more information on what counts as a 1-teaspoon serving of oil, go to mypyramid.gov.

Day	Amount Eaten: Oils
Day 1	_____ teaspoons
Day 2	_____ teaspoons
Day 3	_____ teaspoons
Total three-day intake	_____ teaspoons
Average daily intake	_____ teaspoons (total intake divided by 3)
Recommended intake	_____ teaspoons (from table earlier in this chapter)

Compare your average daily intake to the recommended intake. How many more or fewer teaspoons of oil should you be eating?

_____ teaspoons

As you can probably see from the chart and from your oil intake, it is not difficult to consume enough oils.

Remember that oil is not the same as solid fat. The oils included in the food pyramid contain primarily polyunsaturated and monounsaturated fatty acids and are sources of essential fatty acids. Solid fats such as lard, shortening, butter, margarine containing trans fat, and tropical oils (palm, coconut) contain primarily saturated fatty acids. You should limit your intake of these fats.

Worksheet 7: Food Record Summary

Fill in the following chart by using the information from Worksheets 1 through 6.

Food Group	Recommended Intake	Actual Intake
Grains	_____ ounces	_____ ounces
How many ounces were whole-grain or enriched? _____		
Vegetables	_____ cups	_____ cups
Fruits	_____ cups	_____ cups
Milk	_____ cups	_____ cups
How many cups were low-fat or nonfat? _____		
Meat/beans	_____ ounces	_____ ounces
How many ounces were either fish, beans, nuts, seeds, tofu, low-fat or lean meat, or skinless poultry? _____		
Oils	_____ teaspoons	_____ teaspoons

Worksheet 8: Additional Questions

Using your food records and the food labels you saved, answer the following questions:

Do you drink "empty" calories such as soda on a regular basis? (If you are eating a food daily or every other day, that can be considered "on a regular basis.")

_____

_____

_____

Do you eat foods with a lot of added sugar (cake, cookies, candy) on a regular basis?

_____

_____

_____

Do you use butter or other forms of saturated fat (lard, shortening, margarine with trans fat, tropical oils) on a regular basis?

_____

_____

_____

Do you regularly add sauces containing saturated fat to the foods you eat?

_____

_____

_____

Do the processed foods you eat, such as crackers and cookies, contain trans fat?

_____

_____

_____

What is the saturated-fat content of the processed foods you are eating?

_____

_____

_____

You should now have a very clear picture of what you are eating—the good, the bad, and the ugly. The next section will show you how to get less of the ugly and more of the good into your diet.

How to Improve Your Diet

Now that you have compared what you should be eating with what you actually are eating, you can start making changes to improve the nutritional quality of your diet. By taking a critical look at your food record, you have identified where you should make adjustments in your eating. You may have found that you need to increase or decrease servings from the various food groups. For example, you may be consuming too many ounces of meat and not enough cups of vegetables. If so, you need to increase your vegetable intake and decrease your meat intake.

To help maintain an appropriate intake of calories, it is important that when adding food to your meal plan, you take something else away, assuming you are now eating enough. For example, if you need to increase your fruit and milk intake but are on target with the other food groups, you will need to look at your intake of discretionary calories. These are calories you need to maintain your weight but don't necessarily need for nutrients. Foods such as soda, potato chips, sauces, butter, and cookies can be considered sources of discretionary calories. To avoid consuming too many calories, you may need to decrease the amount you eat of foods high in fat and sugar.

Personal Viewpoint

I am not a fan of "fakes." In my opinion, it is preferable to consume small amounts of butter, cane sugar, and bacon than margarine, Splenda, or imitation bacon bits, even if the sugar or saturated-fat content is higher.

Adding Fruit to Your Diet

If you are like many, your food record indicates that you have to eat more fruit. To get started, make a list of all the fruits you like and some new ones you are willing to try. Then list all the creative ways you can easily incorporate these fruits into your meals. Here are some suggestions:

* Add chopped dried papaya or apricots to breakfast cereal.
* Mix fresh sliced strawberries into yogurt.
* Top toast or rice cakes with nut butter and sliced banana or apple.
* Top your waffles or pancakes with raspberries, blackberries, or blueberries.
* Add sliced apples or pears to sandwiches.
* Toss sliced pears, strawberries, grapes, or orange segments into salads.

Adding Vegetables to Your Diet

If you are like many, your food record also indicates that you have to eat more vegetables. Again, make a list of all the vegetables you like and some new ones you are willing to try. As with fruit, list the creative ways you can easily incorporate these vegetables into your meals. Here are a few suggestions to get you started:

- ✣ Add leafy greens and sliced tomatoes to all your savory sandwiches.
- ✣ Include a salad of leafy greens and chopped fresh vegetables at every dinner.
- ✣ Add baby carrots, sliced mushrooms, or frozen peas to rice and quinoa. (Add them right to the pot of water when you add the rice or quinoa.)
- ✣ Include asparagus, zucchini, or mushrooms in your pasta sauces.
- ✣ Make a weekly pot of vegetable-based chili or soup.
- ✣ Make some basil or spinach pesto, and add it to sandwiches, chicken dishes, or pasta.

Adding Gluten-Free Whole Grains to Your Diet

You may not be familiar with (much less have tried) the gluten-free whole grains quinoa, amaranth, buckwheat, millet, teff, or sorghum. Nonetheless, these grains really are delicious and easy to cook and bake with. See Chapter 6 for delicious recipes incorporating gluten-free whole grains. To familiarize yourself with these grains, you may want to take the following advice:

- ✣ Each week, choose a new grain to experiment with. If you like to bake, purchase a small bag of flour as well as a small box of the whole grain or seed. Many producers of gluten-free whole grains sell starter packs to help consumers experiment with their products. See Appendix C for retail sources of whole grains.
- ✣ Cook the grain, using the recipe provided on the side of the box. Or use a basic pilaf recipe, using the new grain you are trying in place of the rice. For added flavor, use gluten-free chicken or vegetable stock in place of water.
- ✣ Spend some time really tasting the cooked grain, thinking about what flavors and foods it would go well with.

❖ If you like to bake, try substituting the new flour for whatever flour you usually use when baking bread, muffins, or baked goods. Again, spend some time really tasting the baked good, thinking about what flavors it would go well with.

Sample Meal Plans

The following meal ideas are provided to give you an idea of the healthful options available to you. For many more suggestions for appetizers, entrees, side dishes, desserts, and snacks, see the recipes in Chapter 6.

BREAKFAST SUGGESTIONS

❖ Two whole-grain gluten-free rice cakes topped with peanut butter and sliced banana, served with low-fat milk
❖ Low-fat yogurt mixed with gluten-free enriched or whole-grain cereal, served with orange juice
❖ Poached egg on toast, using gluten-free enriched bread or whole-grain waffle, served with low-fat milk and dried apricots
❖ Gluten-free enriched bagel topped with low-fat ricotta cheese and sliced strawberries, served with cranberry juice
❖ Whole-grain hot cereal topped with maple syrup and raisins, served with low-fat milk
❖ Gluten-free whole-grain waffle topped with maple syrup and blueberries, served with low-fat milk

LUNCH SUGGESTIONS

❖ Turkey club served on gluten-free enriched or homemade whole-grain bread, served with a piece of fruit and seltzer water
❖ Black-bean and cheese quesadilla made with whole-grain corn tortillas and topped with tomato and red onion slices and salsa, served with seltzer water

❖ Whole-grain gluten-free rice cakes topped with peanut butter and jelly, served with a piece of fruit and glass of low-fat milk

❖ Chopped salad made with lettuce, tomato, avocado, red onion, and corn, topped with oil and vinegar dressing, served with whole-grain rice crackers and low-fat milk

❖ Whole-grain gluten-free flatbread topped with hummus, served with tomato-mozzarella salad and seltzer water

❖ Open-faced grilled cheese and tomato sandwich, served on an enriched gluten-free bagel with baked beans and seltzer water

Dinner Suggestions

❖ Pizza made with ready-made gluten-free enriched pizza crust topped with tomato sauce, low-fat cheese, and vegetables, served with cranberry juice mixed with seltzer water

❖ Pasta with pesto sauce made with whole-grain or enriched gluten-free noodles and topped with Parmesan cheese, served with seltzer water and lime

❖ Grilled chicken, quinoa, and sautéed vegetables, served with low-fat milk

❖ Tacos made with whole-grain corn tortillas and filled with black beans, low-fat cheese, and diced vegetables, served with Spanish rice (using whole-grain or enriched white rice) and seltzer water

❖ Grilled salmon served over sautéed greens with oven-roasted red potatoes, served with low-fat milk

❖ Vegetarian chili made with a variety of beans and vegetables, served with homemade tortilla chips (toss sliced corn tortillas with olive oil and salt and bake) and seltzer water with lime

Snack Suggestions

❖ Gluten-free energy/sports bars such as Lara or Genisoy brands (check labels, as not all are gluten free)

- Sliced banana and peanut butter
- Popcorn tossed with raisins and nuts
- Rice crackers topped with low-fat cheese and chopped olives
- Homemade tortilla chips served with salsa and avocado
- Fruit smoothie made with low-fat yogurt and berries

6

Recipes for Enjoying Gluten-Free Food

Omit and substitute! That's how recipes should be written. Please don't ever get so hung up on published recipes that you forget you can omit and substitute.

—Jeff Smith (The Frugal Gourmet)

SOME OF THE recipes in this chapter are my personal favorites. They use simple ingredients, are easy to prepare, and pack the nutritional punch that will keep you healthy on a gluten-free diet. Many of these recipes were contributed by colleagues of mine, including dietitians, and national support group leaders who specialize in celiac disease and the gluten-free diet. Some of these recipes were contributed by mothers who cook for children with celiac disease and friends who have cooked gluten-free meals for me. Here's to healthful and delicious gluten-free eating!

Ingredients such as garbanzo bean flour, amaranth, quinoa, buckwheat, millet, teff, sorghum, wild rice, and bean flours called for in some of these recipes may be available in your local natural-foods store. If not, they may be ordered from several companies. Please see Appendix C for mail-order sources.

Breakfast

Buckwheat Pancakes

The flavor of buckwheat just goes with maple syrup, so buckwheat flour makes terrific pancakes. Make sure the flour is 100 percent buckwheat.

  1 cup buckwheat flour
  2 tablespoons cornstarch
  ½ teaspoon salt
  1 teaspoon baking soda
  1 cup orange juice
  ¼ cup maple syrup
  Oil for cooking

Preheat a stovetop grill pan or skillet over medium heat.

In a medium-size mixing bowl, combine the buckwheat flour, cornstarch, salt, and baking soda. Add the orange juice and maple syrup, and combine.

Put a small amount of oil on the grill or skillet. Ladle enough batter onto the grill to make 4- to 5-inch pancakes. Cook until the edges of the pancakes start to look dry. Flip pancakes, and cook for an additional minute. Serve with maple syrup, fruit preserves, or a bit of honey butter.

Makes 8 to 10 pancakes

Teff Hot Cereal

If you like hot cereal, then you may want to give this nutritious recipe a try. Cooked teff grain has a nice nutty, chewy texture and a mild flavor.

¾ cup water
¼ cup uncooked teff grain
¼ cup raisins (or any other dried fruit)
1 tablespoon unsweetened dried coconut
1 tablespoon yogurt
1 tablespoon maple syrup

In a small saucepan, bring water to a boil. Add teff and raisins. Cover and reduce heat to low (maintain simmer). Cook until all the water is absorbed. Top with coconut, yogurt, and maple syrup

Makes 1 serving

Cynthia's Sorghum, Fruit, and Nut Treat

This recipe is courtesy of Cynthia Kupper, RD, a nutritionist and the executive director of the Gluten Intolerance Group of North America. It's one of Cynthia's favorite recipes—easy but great, a wonderfully nutritious snack or breakfast cereal. Sorghum grain is cooked the same way as rice and can be cooked overnight in a slow cooker or rice cooker. Cooked sorghum can be stored covered in the refrigerator for three to five days for a fast addition to any meal.

> 1 cup whole white sorghum, cooked
> 2 tablespoons whole blanched almonds
> ¼ cup dried or fresh blueberries or cranberries
> Dash of cinnamon or freshly grated nutmeg
> 1 tablespoon maple syrup (optional)

Cook sorghum until tender according to instructions on package. Add almonds and berries. Top with cinnamon or nutmeg and maple syrup, if desired. Serve warm. For variety, substitute other favorite fruits, nuts, and spices.

Makes 1 serving

Lunch

*A*nne's Piecrust for Savory Fillings

This recipe is courtesy of Anne Lee, M.S. Ed., RD, nutritionist at the Celiac Disease Center at Columbia University. This piecrust is great for savory pies such as spinach pie and quiche. The recipe calls for nut meal. You can purchase this ingredient at natural-foods stores or make your own using a coffee grinder.

1 cup ground nut meal, such as almond or hazelnut
2 tablespoons garbanzo bean flour (also known as chick-pea flour)
¼ cup butter

Mix together nut meal, flour, and butter. The mixture should have the consistency of a graham cracker crust. Press the mixture into a pie plate. Fill as desired.

Makes 1 crust

Favorite Sandwich Spread

When you think of a sandwich, beans probably do not come to mind. But believe it or not, they make a delicious sandwich spread. This recipe calls for chick-peas, which are my favorite bean, but any bean you like will work.

1 19-ounce can chick-peas, drained
Juice of 1 lemon
1 clove garlic, finely chopped (use more or less to taste)
Salt to taste
3 cups loosely packed fresh basil, rinsed well and dried
¼ cup pine nuts, walnuts, or pecans
2 cloves garlic, peeled
2 tablespoons extra-virgin olive oil
6 corn tortillas, warmed
2 medium tomatoes, diced
1 small sweet (Vidalia) onion, diced

In a medium bowl, using a potato masher, mash the chick-peas to desired consistency. Add the juice of 1 lemon, chopped garlic, and salt to taste. Mix to combine. Set aside.

In a blender or food processor, place the basil, nuts, garlic cloves, olive oil, and salt to taste. Blend until you have a thick but smooth sauce. Spread a thin layer of the basil mixture on each warm tortilla. Layer the bean mixture, tomato, and onion on one end of each tortilla. Roll up and enjoy!

Makes 6 roll-ups

Sweet and Savory Rice Cakes

Believe it or not, there are many tasty treats you can make with rice cakes.

Betsy's Tuna Melt

My mom loves tuna melts. In fact, she has been known to get excited when she spots a tuna melt on a restaurant menu. This recipe is how she eats her tuna melts these days.

1 6-ounce can water-packed light tuna, drained
1 tablespoon minced onion
1 tablespoon mayonnaise
⅛ teaspoon mustard (check labels)
Salt to taste
Pepper to taste
4 rice cakes (check labels)
4 slices low-fat cheddar cheese

Mix together tuna, onion, mayonnaise, mustard, salt, and pepper. Spread on rice cakes, and top each with a cheese slice. Heat under broiler until cheese melts.

Variations: Add chopped dill pickle or celery to the tuna mixture; place a tomato slice under the cheese slice; or sprinkle Italian herbs on top of the cheese.

Important note: Many rice cake packages advise against heating rice cakes, although we have never experienced a problem when doing so.

Makes 4 tuna melts

Gluten-Free S'Mores

About the only thing I remember from my Girl Scout days is s'mores. While this version isn't quite like the original, they are still simple and delicious and incorporate the chocolate, marshmallow, and crunch! This is not really a lunch item, but while we're on the topic of rice cakes . . .

    2 marshmallows (check labels)
    1 chocolate-flavored rice cake (check labels)

Roast marshmallows (preferably on a stick over a campfire). Place roasted marshmallows on a chocolate rice cake. Yummy!

Makes 1 s'more

Dinner

Black-Bean Tacos

Tacos are a great party food and a terrific way to boost your intake of beans and vegetables. Place each ingredient in a separate serving bowl, and let everyone assemble his or her own taco.

1 19-ounce can black beans, rinsed and drained
Salt to taste
1 avocado, mashed
Juice of 1 lime
8 corn taco shells (enriched or whole-grain)
4 ounces low-fat Monterey Jack cheese, grated
1 medium onion, chopped
20 pitted kalamata olives, halved
1 medium tomato, diced
1 roasted red pepper (from a jar is fine), diced
Taco sauce

Heat the beans in a small saucepan with enough water to just cover the beans. Add salt to taste. Bring the beans to a boil, and simmer until almost all the water is absorbed.

Mix the avocado with the lime juice.

Heat the taco shells in the oven according to package instructions.

To assemble the tacos, layer the beans, cheese, onion, olives, tomato, and red pepper in the shells. Top with avocado and taco sauce.

Makes 8 tacos

Brown-Rice Pasta with Tomato and Portobello Mushroom Sauce

Red pasta sauces are a great way to incorporate more vegetables into your diet. This recipe calls for mushrooms, but you could just as easily use bell pepper, broccoli, or asparagus. A splash of your favorite red wine will liven up the sauce.

2 tablespoons olive oil
2 garlic cloves, finely chopped
1 medium onion, chopped
1 7-ounce jar pitted kalamata olives, coarsely chopped
4 portobello mushroom caps, sliced and then diced
1 28-ounce can crushed tomatoes
1 6-ounce can tomato paste
1 teaspoon dried basil or to taste
1 teaspoon dried oregano or to taste
Dash of crushed red pepper or to taste
Salt and pepper to taste
½ pound gluten-free whole-grain brown-rice pasta, cooked
    according to package directions
½ cup grated Parmesan cheese

Heat olive oil in a large skillet; sauté the garlic and onion over medium heat until softened. Add the olives and mushrooms, stirring to mix. Add the crushed tomatoes and tomato paste. Stir in the basil, oregano, and crushed red pepper. Season with salt and pepper. Bring to a boil, and simmer, stirring frequently, for approximately 30 minutes or until ready to serve. Serve over pasta, and top with grated Parmesan.

Makes 4 servings

Black-Bean and Corn Tortilla Bake

This dish is a true one-pot meal. It takes only a few minutes to prepare, and then you can pop it in the oven and forget about it for the next fifty minutes.

12 whole-grain corn tortillas
2 19-ounce cans black beans, rinsed and drained
1 medium yellow onion, diced
¾ cup frozen corn
1 red bell pepper, diced
1 green bell pepper, diced
1 cup shredded cooked chicken
4 ounces low-fat Monterey Jack cheese, grated
1 medium tomato, diced
1 avocado, diced
Gluten-free salsa

Preheat oven to 350°F. In a shallow medium-sized baking dish, arrange a layer of 4 tortillas, then top with one-third of the black beans, onion, corn, red and green peppers, chicken, and cheese. Repeat with two more layers of each ingredient.

Cover tightly with aluminum foil, and bake 50 minutes. Let the dish set 5 minutes before serving. Top each portion with tomato, avocado, and salsa.

Makes 4 servings

Pam's Quinoa Primavera

*This recipe is courtesy of Pam Cureton, RD, LDN, nutritionist at
the Center for Celiac Research, University of Maryland School of
Medicine, in Baltimore. It is a great alternative to pasta primavera.
Pam says the secret is in the dressing. The vegetables can be modified
to your liking. Experiment!*

> 4 cups cooked quinoa
> ½ cup diced green olives
> ½ cup diced assorted bell peppers
> ½ cup chopped cooked asparagus
> ½ cup chopped raw broccoli
> ¼ cup diced gluten-free pepperoni
> 1 medium tomato, chopped
> ½ cup any other vegetable or meat of your choice
> Salt to taste
> Pepper to taste

> DRESSING
> 2 cups gluten-free balsamic vinegar dressing
> Or mix together:
> 1 cup balsamic vinegar
> 1 cup extra-virgin olive oil

Mix together all ingredients, adding the dressing last. Allow
to marinate at least 1 hour (or overnight) before serving.

Makes 10 to 12 servings (½ cup each)

Alice's Seafood Cakes

This recipe is courtesy of Alice Miller, who cooks delicious, completely gluten-free meals for her friends. I know these cakes are absolutely delicious, because I have been lucky enough to have Alice make them for me. Alice recommends using organic ingredients whenever possible.

2 cups fish stock
1 cup uncooked brown rice
1 cup crabmeat, picked over for cartilage
2 ears fresh uncooked corn, with kernels cut off (or 2 cups frozen corn, thawed)
½ cup diced red bell pepper
½ cup diced red onion
½ cup diced celery
1 tablespoon Old Bay seasoning
4 turns freshly ground black pepper
1 tablespoon ground coriander
1 tablespoon Dijon mustard (check labels)
1 tablespoon lemon juice
1 tablespoon lemon zest
2 eggs, beaten
1 cup diced fish (salmon or cod)
1 cup coarsely chopped cilantro
¼ cup canola oil for sautéing

Bring the fish stock to a boil, and add the rice. Reduce heat, and cook until tender, about 20 minutes. Let cool.

Meanwhile, in a fine mesh strainer, place a paper towel and the crabmeat, and let drain 15 minutes. In a large bowl, mix the corn, red pepper, onion, celery, Old Bay seasoning, pepper, coriander, mustard, lemon juice, and zest. When the rice is cool, add to bowl, and mix with the eggs, crabmeat, fish, and ¾ cup cilantro. With your hands, take about ½ cup of the mixture, form it into a cake, and place each cake onto sheets of paper towels.

Heat oil in a nonstick skillet. When hot, sauté cakes on each side for about 3 to 5 minutes.

Cakes can be made ahead of time and refrigerated. Then they can be reheated by sautéing them again or by placing them in a 400°F oven until heated through.

Serve with sliced lemon and/or aioli, and sprinkle with remaining chopped cilantro.

Makes 16 cakes

Melinda's Amaranth and Brown-Rice-Stuffed Red Peppers

*This recipe is courtesy of Melinda Dennis, M.S., RD, LDN, nutrition coordinator at the Celiac Center, Beth Israel Deaconess Medical Center, in Boston. (Visit Melinda's website at deletethewheat.com.) Inspired by "The Complete Guide to Fast Cook Grains" by Dana Jacobi (*Natural Health, *March/April 1995), this vegetarian dish is filling, and you can easily modify it by substituting in your favorite chopped vegetables, dried fruit (dates, apricots), nuts and seeds, spices and herbs (oregano, dill), and grains (millet, quinoa).*

¼ cup uncooked amaranth seed
½ cup uncooked brown rice
2¼ cups gluten-free vegetable broth or water
1 tablespoon plus ¼ cup olive oil
1 onion, finely chopped
2 garlic cloves, minced
1 cup corn kernels, freshly cooked or frozen and defrosted
1 cup button mushrooms (stems removed), chopped
½ cup chopped cashews or other nuts (plain, unsalted)
2 teaspoons lime juice
2 tablespoons sunflower seeds
½ cup raisins
¾ cup canned black beans, drained
1 tablespoon chopped fresh basil
1 tablespoon chopped fresh oregano
2 tablespoons chopped fresh cilantro
Salt and ground black pepper to taste
6 medium red bell peppers, tops removed, seeded and
   ribbed
½ cup marinara sauce (check labels for gluten)

Preheat oven to 375°F. Cook amaranth and rice with vegetable broth or water in a rice cooker, or bring broth or water to a boil in a saucepan, add amaranth and rice, and cook until tender. Add water as needed until rice is soft. Cool in a large bowl.

Heat 1 tablespoon olive oil in a skillet, and sauté onion and garlic until translucent.

In a bowl, mix the corn, mushrooms, cashews, lime juice, sunflower seeds, raisins, black beans, basil, oregano, cilantro, black pepper, and salt.

Thinly slice the bottom of each pepper (without making any holes) to make a flat bottom so that it can stand up. Fill each pepper with one-sixth of the vegetable and nut mixture. Lightly brush the top of each pepper with the remaining ¼ cup olive oil. Place the peppers in a pan, and fill the pan with 1 inch of water. Bake, uncovered, for about 1 hour or until the peppers are soft when pierced with a knife.

Pour a spoonful of warmed marinara sauce, pasta sauce, or other sauce of your choice over the peppers before serving.

Makes 6 servings

Betsy's Santa Fe Chicken with Rice and Beans

This recipe is courtesy of my mom, Betsy Spurr, and is dedicated to my dad, Robert Spurr. This recipe was inspired by many restaurant meals my parents ate while vacationing in Santa Fe, New Mexico. This recipe calls for liquid smoke; most varieties should be gluten free, but check labels just to be sure.

3 tablespoons lime juice (fresh or bottled)
1 tablespoon liquid smoke
4 boneless, skinless chicken breasts
1 cup uncooked brown rice
2¼ cups water or gluten-free chicken or vegetable broth (optional)
1 19-ounce can black beans, drained
¼ cup water
1 clove garlic, minced
1 small onion, chopped
2 tablespoons olive oil
2 medium tomatoes, chopped
Sour cream to taste

Mix lime juice and liquid smoke in a 9-inch pie plate or baking dish. Place chicken breasts in lime juice marinade, turning once, for 30 minutes.

While chicken is marinating, prepare the rice according to package directions, using broth, if desired, in place of water for added flavor. In a small saucepan, place the beans, water, garlic, and 1 tablespoon of the chopped onion. Simmer until all the water is absorbed. Add black beans to rice, and mix.

Cut marinated chicken into strips. Heat olive oil in skillet over medium-high heat, and sauté chicken strips until brown. Reduce heat, and cook chicken thoroughly.

To serve, place chicken strips on rice and bean mixture. Garnish with remaining chopped onion, tomatoes, and sour cream.

Makes 4 servings

Emily's Fish Sticks

This recipe is courtesy of Jane Roberts, who like her three children, Andrew, Emily, and Claire, has celiac disease. Thank you also to Jane's sister Carol Shilson, executive director of the University of Chicago Celiac Disease Center, for putting us in touch. This recipe is oh, so, kid friendly!

Juice of 1 lemon
4–6 plain fish fillets, such as tilapia or sole
2 eggs
7 ounces (approximately) corn tortilla chips
1 teaspoon paprika (for color)

Preheat oven to 350°F. Spray a baking sheet lightly with gluten-free nonstick cooking spray.

Squeeze lemon juice over fish fillets, and cut each fillet into strips 4 inches long. Beat eggs in a bowl large enough to dip fillets in. In a food processor or by hand, crush the tortilla chips and paprika.

Dip each fish strip into the eggs, and then roll it in tortilla chip crumbs. When the fish is completely covered, place it on the prepared baking sheet. Bake 7 to 10 minutes or until inside is flaky.

Makes approximately 60 to 70 fish sticks

*C*laire's Balsamic Chicken and Quinoa

This recipe is courtesy of Jane Roberts, who like her three children, Andrew, Emily, and Claire, has celiac disease. Thank you also to Jane's sister Carol Shilson, executive director of the University of Chicago Celiac Disease Center, for putting us in touch. This recipe is a tasty alternative to chicken and rice.

BALSAMIC CHICKEN
1 cup olive oil
½ cup balsamic vinegar
3 tablespoons sugar
3 tablespoons ketchup
1 tablespoon gluten-free Worcestershire sauce
2 medium scallions, diced
1 teaspoon salt
½ teaspoon cracked pepper
1 teaspoon gluten-free dry mustard
1 medium garlic clove, crushed
Tabasco to taste
2 whole boneless, skinless chicken breasts

QUINOA
1 cup uncooked quinoa
2 cups water or gluten-free chicken broth
1 tablespoon plus 1 teaspoon olive oil
1 yellow bell pepper, diced
1 red bell pepper, diced
2 cloves garlic, crushed
1 tablespoon dried basil
¼ cup pine nuts

Mix together a marinade of 1 cup olive oil and the balsamic vinegar, sugar, ketchup, Worcestershire sauce, scallions, salt, cracked pepper, mustard, garlic, and Tabasco. Add chicken, and marinate 1 to 2 hours.

Preheat oven to 350°F. Place marinated chicken in a 13″ × 9″ or 8″ × 8″ baking pan, and bake 30 to 40 minutes until cooked through. Slice into strips, and serve over quinoa.

Boil quinoa 5 to 10 minutes in water or broth to which 1 teaspoon olive oil has been added; reduce heat, and simmer, stirring until fluffy. Add remaining tablespoon of olive oil as needed while stirring. Add yellow and red peppers, garlic, basil, and pine nuts.

Makes 4 servings

Mary's Pork Chop Bake

This recipe is courtesy of Mary Schluckebier, M.A., a home economist and the executive director of the Celiac Sprue Association. This is not your average pork chop and rice recipe! It calls for sweet rice flour, which can be ordered from Bob's Red Mill.

4 pork chops, ¾ inch thick
2 tablespoons drippings or butter
1 small onion, chopped
1 cup cooked brown rice
¾ cup cooked whole-grain sorghum (see note)
4 ounces low-fat cheddar cheese, shredded
1 tablespoon sweet rice flour
1 tablespoon dried parsley
¼ teaspoon gluten-free dry mustard
1 teaspoon salt
¼ teaspoon black pepper

Preheat oven to 350°F. In a hot heavy skillet with a dash of salt or vegetable oil added to prevent sticking, brown pork chops on each side. Remove chops and drain all but 2 tablespoons of drippings, or add butter. Add onion and sauté lightly.

Transfer onion to a large bowl; add the rice, sorghum, and cheese. In a smaller bowl, mix the rice flour, parsley, mustard, salt, and pepper. Add to the onion and rice mixture. Spread the onion and rice mixture in a shallow baking dish large enough to allow the edges of the chops to touch without overcrowding; top with the pork chops. Cover with a tight-fitting lid, and bake 35 minutes. (If the dish is not covered tightly, you may need to add some additional liquid while baking.) Pork is considered done when it reaches an internal temperature of 160°F.

Note: To cook sorghum for this dish, soak a rounded ½ cup whole-grain sorghum in 2 cups water overnight. Drain and discard the liquid. Bring 2 cups water to a boil, add the soaked grain, and boil 20 minutes. Whisk occasionally, so the grain does not stick to the pan. Drain. During the cooking process, the ½ cup grain will swell to approximately ¾ cup.

Makes 4 servings

Pablo's Quinoa Pasta with Feta and Asparagus

This recipe is courtesy of Andrea Levario, J.D., executive director of the American Celiac Disease Alliance and mother of a son with celiac disease. It is quick, easy, and tasty!

2 cups cooked quinoa pasta (macaroni or fusilli)
9 tablespoons olive oil
½ pound medium shrimp, peeled and deveined, tail on
½ teaspoon minced garlic
¼ teaspoon cumin
¼ pound of asparagus, washed, trimmed to 1½-inch pieces
¼ pound feta cheese, crumbled
Pepper to taste

Cook pasta according to package instructions. Drain and toss lightly in a large bowl with 1 tablespoon olive oil. Set aside.

Wash shrimp. Place in medium bowl with garlic and cumin. Add 2 tablespoons olive oil. Toss together. Set aside.

Heat 3 tablespoons olive oil in a medium skillet. Add asparagus, and sauté over medium heat 3 to 4 minutes, or until just tender. Remove from heat, and place asparagus in a small bowl. Return skillet to medium heat. Add 3 tablespoons olive oil and shrimp mixture. Cook 4 to 5 minutes or until the shrimp are no longer translucent.

Top pasta with shrimp and asparagus; top with feta. Add pepper to taste.

Makes 4 servings

Natalie's Ukrainian Stuffed Cabbage

This recipe is courtesy of Natalie Mazurets, M.S., RD, a nutritionist who has celiac disease. It is a traditional Ukrainian stuffed-cabbage recipe that was passed down from Natalie's grandmother to her mother and then to her. Natalie's grandmother told her that in the Ukraine, people ate only what they could grow or raise on their own farms. That included fruits, vegetables, and meat. They canned, pickled, or smoked whatever they could, so food would be available in the winter. This recipe includes the most common staples available to people on the farm. This is one of Natalie's favorite meals, and luckily for her (and us), it has always been gluten free.

    1 large head cabbage
    2 cups uncooked brown rice
    ½ cup uncooked buckwheat
    ¼ cup salted butter
    1 large yellow onion, chopped
    3 cloves garlic, minced
    1 16-ounce can tomato sauce (unseasoned)
    Salt to taste
    Pepper to taste
    1 pound ground pork or beef
    1 16-ounce can stewed tomatoes

Boil the entire head of cabbage until tender. Set aside and allow to cool. Prepare the rice and buckwheat according to package directions. Set aside.

Preheat oven to 350°F. Melt butter in a medium skillet, and sauté onion and garlic.

Mix together in a large bowl the rice, buckwheat, onions, and garlic. Add ½ can of tomato sauce, the salt and pepper, and the uncooked meat. Mix again.

Separate the cabbage leaves. Line a large, deep baking pan with cabbage leaves, using any leaves that may have broken during boiling. If no leaves broke, use the thinnest leaves, which will not be durable for rolling.

To prepare the cabbage rolls, stuff each cabbage leaf with enough of the mixture that it appears to fill the leaf when rolled. (The amount will vary as the size of the cabbage leaf varies.) Place the stuffing at the end of the leaf where it is the thickest. Roll the cabbage leaf to the opposite end, folding in the sides to keep the stuffing inside. Place the rolled cabbage leaf in the baking pan. When all the leaves are rolled and stacked in the pan, pour the remaining tomato sauce with ½ cup water over the cabbage rolls. Spread the stewed tomatoes over the top. Top with any excess cabbage leaves. Cover and bake 1 hour.

Serve with tomato sauce, gravy, or sour cream.

Makes approximately 25 stuffed leaves, depending on the size of the cabbage

Natalie's Baked Salmon Burgers

This recipe is courtesy of Natalie Mazurets, M.S., RD, a nutritionist with celiac disease. It is a modified version of a recipe developed by Natalie's father when she was a child. When Natalie first started making these burgers, she added fresh vegetables. When she was diagnosed with celiac disease, she had to find a substitute for bread crumbs and decided on a combination of cornmeal and quinoa flakes. Natalie also suggests making these burgers with canned tuna.

½ medium green bell pepper
½ medium onion
1 medium carrot, peeled
1 14¾-ounce can pink salmon
1 large egg
¼ teaspoon paprika (or to taste)
¼ teaspoon black pepper (or to taste)
1 teaspoon parsley
¼ cup mayonnaise
¼ cup whole-grain cornmeal
½ cup quinoa flakes
1 avocado, mashed until smooth

Preheat oven to 350°F. Chop the bell pepper, onion, and carrot in a food processor. Break up the salmon by mashing it with a fork. In a large bowl, mix the bell pepper, onion, and carrot mixture with the salmon, egg, paprika, black pepper, parsley, mayonnaise, cornmeal, and quinoa flakes. Roll mixture with hands, and form into 3-inch patties about 1 inch thick.

Place patties on a greased cookie sheet or broiling pan, and bake 15 minutes. Flip burgers, and bake an additional 5 minutes or until burgers appear fully cooked. Serve with mashed avocado.

Makes 12 patties

Mary Kay's Pan Pizza

This recipe is courtesy of Mary Kay Sharrett, M.S., RD, clinical dietitian at Children's Hospital in Columbus, Ohio, and founder and dietitian advisor to the Gluten Free Gang, a celiac support group of central Ohio. She received a version of this recipe more than twenty years ago. Pizza is a fun way to eat vegetables, but tasty gluten-free crusts can be difficult to find. The crust is based on whole-grain brown rice, which you can find in any grocery store. Some toppings are suggested, but any will do. Experiment!

    1 cup uncooked brown rice
    3 cups grated part-skim mozzarella cheese
    1 egg, slightly beaten
    2 cups tomato sauce
    1 teaspoon garlic powder
    1 teaspoon dried oregano
    1 teaspoon dried basil
    1 small onion, chopped
    1 red bell pepper, diced
    1 green bell pepper, diced
    ½ cup mushrooms, sliced
    ½ cup grated Parmesan cheese

Preheat oven to 425°F. Lightly oil a 12″ round or 11″ × 19″ rectangular pizza pan or an 11″ × 13″ shallow baking dish.

Prepare the rice as directed on package. Immediately after the rice is cooked, add 1 cup of the mozzarella and egg. Stir well to blend all ingredients and melt the cheese. Spread rice mixture evenly on greased pan. Bake 15 minutes only, and remove crust from oven.

Spread tomato sauce evenly over crust, and sprinkle with garlic powder, oregano, and basil. Arrange onion, peppers, and mushrooms evenly over the top. Top with the remaining moz-zarella and Parmesan cheeses. Return pizza to oven, and bake an additional 5 minutes or until the sauce is hot and the cheese is melted. Let the pizza sit for 5 minutes before cutting.

Makes 1 pizza

Side Dishes

*B*rown-Rice Pilaf with Carrots and Mushrooms

Brown rice is just as easy to cook as white rice with the added benefits of being tastier and more healthful. You can use brown rice in a basic pilaf recipe, or jazz it up as I have done here by adding carrots and mushrooms (or any other chopped vegetable) after you add the broth.

  2 tablespoons olive oil
  1 small yellow onion, chopped
  2 tablespoons pine nuts
  ½ ounce gluten-free brown-rice spaghetti (or vermicelli if
      you can find it), broken into 1-inch pieces
  1 cup uncooked brown rice
  2¼ cups gluten-free chicken or vegetable broth (or 1 14-
      ounce can broth plus ½ cup water)
  6 baby carrots, chopped
  10 button mushrooms, sliced

Heat olive oil in a medium-size saucepan or covered skillet; add onion and sauté over medium heat until softened. Add the pine nuts, spaghetti, and rice, and brown lightly. Stir in the broth (and water if needed). Add the carrots and mushrooms. Bring to a boil. Cover and reduce heat. Simmer until all the water has been absorbed.

Makes 4 servings

Tomato, Mozzarella, Basil, and Quinoa Salad

Quinoa is one of the easiest alternative grains to use. If you can cook rice, you can cook quinoa.

1 cup uncooked quinoa
2 cups gluten-free chicken or vegetable broth
2 medium tomatoes, seeded and diced
4 ounces fresh mozzarella, diced
½ cup loosely packed fresh basil leaves, sliced into strips
1 tablespoon olive oil
1 garlic clove, minced
Salt to taste

Cook the quinoa according to package instructions, substituting the broth for water called for on the package.

While the quinoa is cooking, mix together the tomatoes, mozzarella, basil, olive oil, garlic, and salt in a large bowl. Serve the salad mixture over the warm quinoa.

Makes 4 servings

Caramelized Onions and Zucchini over Quinoa

Quinoa is a great grain to use when cooking foods with strong flavors. This is because quinoa doesn't have a strong flavor of its own but takes on the flavor of whatever it is cooked with.

   2 tablespoons olive oil
   1 large yellow onion, diced
   1 large zucchini, thinly sliced
   1 cup uncooked quinoa
   2 cups gluten-free chicken or vegetable broth
   ¼ cup grated Parmesan cheese
   Salt and pepper to taste

In a large skillet (not nonstick), heat the olive oil over medium to medium-high heat. Sauté the onion and zucchini, stirring frequently, until the vegetables are nicely browned.

In the meantime, cook the quinoa according to package instructions, substituting chicken broth for water called for on the package. Serve the onion and zucchini mixture over the quinoa. Sprinkle with Parmesan, salt, and pepper.

Makes 4 servings as a side dish

Bean and Kasha Salad

Kasha (roasted buckwheat groats) has a nutty flavor that works well with beans.

>   1½ cups cooked kasha
>   1 large tomato, diced
>   1 small red onion, diced
>   2 tablespoons chopped flat-leaf parsley
>   1 19-ounce can dark-red kidney beans, rinsed and drained
>   2 to 3 tablespoons raspberry-flavored balsamic vinegar (or any other gluten-free flavored vinegar you like)

Prepare the kasha according to package directions. Let it cool slightly. In a large bowl, combine the tomato, onion, parsley, and kidney beans. Add the kasha and vinegar, stirring to combine. Serve warm or cold.

Makes 4 servings as a side dish

Brown Rice, Kasha, and Wild Rice Medley

One of the best ways to become familiar with new grains is to add them to your rice dishes. Kasha (roasted buckwheat groats) and wild rice go particularly well with brown rice. Both kasha and wild rice generally are carried by natural-foods stores.

2 tablespoons olive oil
1 small onion, diced
½ cup pecan halves
½ cup uncooked brown rice
¼ cup uncooked kasha
¼ cup uncooked wild rice
2¼ cups gluten-free chicken or vegetable broth
Salt and pepper to taste
¼ cup diced dried apricots

Heat oil in a medium-size covered skillet over medium-low heat; add the onion and pecans, and sauté until the onions are translucent and the pecans are slightly browned. Add the brown rice, kasha, and wild rice, stirring to combine. Pour in the broth. Add the salt and pepper.

Increase heat to high until the mixture comes to a boil. Reduce heat to low (maintain a simmer), cover, and cook until all the liquid has been absorbed. Top with dried apricots.

Makes 4 servings as a side dish

Elizabeth's Quinoa Pilaf

This recipe is courtesy of Elizabeth Di Biase, RD, who is gluten intolerant. She makes eating fun and exciting by developing her own recipes in which gluten-free grains are combined with foods and spices that are naturally gluten free. Elizabeth says this recipe is very flexible, and she often improvises and changes the amounts and types of spices and seeds to suit her taste. If you want a Mediterranean flavor, she recommends using oregano, extra garlic, and fresh parsley in place of the cumin, cinnamon, and cilantro.

3 tablespoons olive oil (more if the pilaf seems dry)
2 to 3 large garlic cloves, minced
3 to 4 green onions, sliced up to light-green stem
1 large carrot, minced
1 tablespoon sesame seeds
1 tablespoon sunflower seeds
1 tablespoon pumpkin seeds (optional)
1 to 2 teaspoons cumin
¼ teaspoon cinnamon
2 cups cooked quinoa
1 tablespoon fresh lemon juice
1 teaspoon salt, or to taste
Fresh cilantro, chopped
Lemon wedges

OTHER ADD-INS (IF DESIRED)
1 to 2 tablespoons ground flax meal
¼ cup raisins
Sun-dried tomatoes in oil, chopped

Heat olive oil in a large skillet; add garlic, green onions, and carrot, and sauté over medium-low heat for 2–3 minutes. Add sesame seeds, sunflower seeds, and pumpkin seeds (if desired);

sauté 1 minute. Add cumin, cinnamon, and cooked quinoa. Stir until well combined. Turn off heat, and add lemon juice and salt. Garnish with cilantro and lemon wedges. If adding ground flax meal, add with the seeds. If adding raisins, stir in after cooking along with the lemon juice and salt. If adding sun-dried tomatoes, stir in after cooking along with the lemon juice and salt.

Makes 6 servings as a side dish, 4 as a main dish

Trisha's Slow-Cooker Quinoa

This high-fiber recipe is courtesy of Trisha Lyons, RD, a nutritionist specializing in celiac disease at the MetroHealth Medical Center in Cleveland, Ohio. The recipe may be used as an entree or a side dish. Additional vegetables may be added as desired.

2 tablespoons extra-virgin olive oil
½ cup chopped onion
¼ cup chopped green bell pepper
½ cup finely chopped celery
1 14-ounce can diced tomatoes
1 14-ounce can cannellini or black beans, rinsed
2 cups gluten-free chicken broth
1 cup uncooked quinoa, rinsed thoroughly or prewashed
½ teaspoon salt or to taste
¼ teaspoon black pepper or to taste
½ teaspoon oregano
3 cloves garlic, minced
½ cup grated Parmesan cheese

Place olive oil, onion, green pepper, and celery into slow cooker, and cook 15 to 20 minutes on high power. Add tomatoes, beans, broth, quinoa, salt, pepper, oregano, and garlic. Stir until thoroughly mixed. Cover, and reduce heat to low. Cook 2 to 3 hours until ingredients are tender. Top with Parmesan cheese.

Makes 4 servings as a side dish

*M*ark's Quinbouli

This recipe is courtesy of Mark Dinga, M. Ed., RD, LDN, a nutritionist at the University of Pittsburgh Medical Center. This gluten-free version of tabbouleh replaces bulgur wheat with quinoa.

SALAD
1 cup uncooked quinoa
6 cups chopped fresh curly parsley (stems removed)
1 cup grape tomatoes cut in half
1 cup (approximately 4 to 5) sliced mini cucumbers (pickle type)

DRESSING
¼ cup olive oil
Juice of 2 lemons
2 tablespoons rice vinegar
1 tablespoon minced garlic
Salt and pepper to taste

Cook quinoa according to package directions, and set aside to cool. Once cool, toss quinoa with parsley, tomatoes, and cucumbers.

Whisk together dressing ingredients, and combine with vegetables. Chill for at least one hour. Serve with rice crackers.

Makes 8 servings as a side salad

Soups and Chili

Vegetarian Chili with Baked Corn Tortilla Strips

Chili is an easy and delicious way to incorporate more beans and vegetables into your diet. Just about any vegetable or dried bean works in chili, so feel free to be creative. You do not have to be precise with this recipe; just make sure to add enough liquid for the chili to simmer without burning. Store-bought tortilla chips are usually loaded with fat. One alternative is to make your own. Besides accompanying the chili, these tortilla strips are great served with hearty soups.

CHILI
¼ cup corn oil
1 medium onion, diced
10 baby carrots, chopped
1 green bell pepper, chopped
1 red bell pepper, chopped
1 zucchini, chopped
1 10-ounce box frozen corn kernels
2 19-ounce cans dark-red kidney beans, rinsed and drained
1 28-ounce can crushed tomatoes
1 cup water (more if necessary)
1 teaspoon garlic powder or to taste
1 teaspoon chili powder or to taste
Tabasco to taste
1 small red onion, diced
Sour cream

TORTILLA STRIPS
2 tablespoons olive oil
Garlic powder to taste

Salt to taste

12 whole-grain corn tortillas, cut into ½-inch strips

In a large stockpot, heat the corn oil over medium heat; add the onion and sauté until softened. Add the carrots, green and red peppers, zucchini, corn, and kidney beans. Stir in the tomatoes and water. Add the garlic powder and chili powder, stirring to mix. Bring chili to a boil, and reduce heat to simmer. Add Tabasco sauce to taste. Simmer at least 1 hour, stirring frequently. To keep from burning, add water as needed.

To make the tortilla strips, preheat oven to 350°F. In a large bowl, combine the olive oil, garlic powder, and salt. Add the tortilla strips, and toss until they are lightly coated with the oil mixture. Spread the tortilla strips on an ungreased cookie sheet in a single layer, and bake until lightly browned.

Top servings of chili with red onion, a tablespoon of sour cream, and tortilla strips.

Makes 4 to 6 servings

Tomato Vegetable Soup with Amaranth Seed

Another great way to familiarize yourself with the gluten-free grains is to add them to soups. This recipe calls for amaranth seed, but you could just as easily substitute teff grain, quinoa, or kasha.

2 tablespoons olive oil
1 yellow onion, diced
2 carrots, chopped
2 stalks celery, sliced into ¼" crescents
1 small zucchini, diced
½ cup frozen peas
½ cup frozen corn
1 19-ounce can dark-red kidney beans
2 cups gluten-free chicken or vegetable broth
2 cups water
1 28-ounce can crushed tomatoes
½ cup uncooked amaranth seed
1 teaspoon garlic powder
½ teaspoon dried oregano
Red pepper flakes, optional
Salt to taste
Black pepper to taste

Heat olive oil in a large stockpot over medium-low heat. Add the onion, carrots, and celery, and sauté 2 to 3 minutes. Stir in the zucchini, peas, corn, and kidney beans. Add the broth, water, and tomatoes, stirring to combine. Mix in the amaranth seed. Add the garlic powder, oregano, pepper flakes, salt, and black pepper. Simmer over medium-low heat for approximately 1 hour.

Makes 6 to 8 servings

Susan's Classic Southwestern Chili

*This recipe is courtesy of Susan Algert, Ph.D., RD, a nutritionist at
the Warren Celiac Center at the University of California, San Diego.
This chili is easy, quick, and nutritious. It incorporates buckwheat or
quinoa—and gluten-free beer!*

1 tablespoon canola or olive oil
1 pound extra-lean ground beef
2 medium onions, chopped
3 garlic cloves, finely chopped
1 28-ounce can whole tomatoes
1 12-ounce bottle gluten-free beer
1 cup corn kernels (fresh or frozen)
1 cup canned kidney beans
1 cup uncooked quinoa or uncooked buckwheat groats
1 cup water
Chilies, seeded and chopped—your choice, depending on
    degree of hotness desired: 2 jalapeño peppers (hot), or 2
    pasilla peppers (mildly hot), or 2 Anaheim peppers (mild)
5 tablespoons chili powder
1 tablespoon cumin
1 teaspoon paprika
1 teaspoon sugar
1 to 2 teaspoons salt, to taste
½ teaspoon freshly ground pepper, or to taste

GARNISH
Shredded low-fat cheddar cheese
Red onion, diced
Avocado, sliced

Heat oil in a 6-quart saucepan. Add the ground beef, onions,
and garlic, and sauté until meat is browned. Stir in the tomatoes,

beer, corn, kidney beans, quinoa or buckwheat, water, chilies, chili powder, cumin, paprika, and sugar. Bring to a boil over medium-high heat. Reduce heat to medium-low, and simmer, uncovered, about 45 minutes to 1 hour. Taste, and season with salt and pepper as desired.

Garnish each serving with cheese, onion, and avocado if desired.

Makes about 8 to 10 cups

*A*lice's Asian Chicken Noodle Soup

This recipe is courtesy of Alice Miller, who cooks delicious and completely gluten-free meals for her friends. According to Alice, this soup will cure any cold. The recipe calls for either brown-rice noodles or buckwheat noodles. If you choose buckwheat noodles, make sure they are made using 100 percent buckwheat flour. Alice also recommends using homemade chicken stock (she is a purist when it comes to cooking), but if you want to use store-bought broth, just make sure it is gluten free.

> 2 tablespoons olive oil
> 1 carrot, chopped
> 1 celery stalk, chopped
> 1 onion, chopped
> ½ teaspoon red pepper flakes
> 2 tablespoons grated fresh ginger
> 2 cloves garlic, chopped
> 2 quarts chicken stock
> 1 pound (approximately) chicken pieces (bone in), such as 2
>   whole legs or 6 wings
> 8 ounces uncooked brown-rice or buckwheat noodles
> 1 13.5-ounce can coconut milk
> ½ cup frozen, shelled edamame
> 1 tablespoon ground coriander
> 1 tablespoon turmeric
> Salt to taste
> Black pepper to taste
> Fresh cilantro for garnish

In a large stockpot, heat oil; add carrot, celery, and onion, and sauté until tender. Add red pepper flakes, ginger, and garlic, and sauté an additional 2 minutes until fragrant. Add stock and chicken, and let come to a boil. Reduce heat and simmer until chicken is cooked through. Take pot off stove, and remove chicken pieces. When cool enough to handle, debone chicken, remove skin, and cut into bite-size pieces. Put pot back on stove, and bring to a boil. Skim off fat as needed. Add noodles and continue to boil until done. When the noodles are done, reduce heat to simmer, and add the coconut milk, chicken, edamame, coriander, and turmeric. Season to taste with salt and freshly ground pepper. Serve in bowls with chopped fresh cilantro.

Makes 4 to 6 servings

Muffins and Quick Breads

Anne's Sorghum and Chick-Pea Banana Bread

Beans don't always have to be eaten whole. Using garbanzo bean flour in baked goods is an easy way to boost your intake of legumes. This recipe is courtesy of Anne Lee, M.S. Ed., RD, a nutritionist at the Celiac Disease Center at Columbia University.

  1 cup garbanzo bean flour (also known as chick-pea flour)
  1 cup sorghum flour
  ½ teaspoon salt
  1 teaspoon baking soda
  1 teaspoon cinnamon
  ½ teaspoon nutmeg
  ½ cup butter
  1 cup sugar
  2 eggs
  1 cup mashed banana (2 to 3 ripe bananas)

Preheat oven to 350°F. Grease a loaf pan.

Sift together the garbanzo bean and sorghum flours, salt, baking soda, cinnamon, and nutmeg. In a large mixing bowl, cream the butter and sugar. To the butter and sugar mixture, add the eggs one at a time, beating after each egg is added. Add the dry ingredients, mixing well. Add the mashed banana, mixing well.

Pour batter into prepared loaf pan. Bake 55 minutes. Test for doneness using a toothpick. If it comes out clean, the bread is done. Cool bread in the pan before removing.

Makes 1 loaf

*N*ancy's Bread Sticks

This recipe is courtesy of Nancy Patin Falini, M.A., RD, LDN, a nutritionist and the author of Gluten-Free Friends: An Activity Book for Kids. *When Nancy first served these bread sticks to her family, they had no idea they were gluten free.*

2½ cups garbanzo bean flour (also called chick-pea flour)
2 tablespoons sugar
1½ teaspoons baking powder
¾ teaspoon salt
½ cup olive oil
½ cup grape juice

Preheat oven to 350°F. In a large mixing bowl, combine the garbanzo bean flour, sugar, baking powder, and salt. Add the olive oil and grape juice, and mix by hand until dough is formed. Place a portion of the dough between both hands, and roll into sticks about 4 inches long.

Bake on an ungreased baking sheet 12 to 15 minutes until the bread sticks are slightly browned. These bread sticks are especially tasty while still warm from the oven.

Makes 24 to 28 bread sticks

Brooklyn's Blueberry-Banana Muffins

These muffins are a favorite of my niece Brooklyn, who eats gluten free, as well as her brother and sisters, who don't have to eat gluten free but sometimes do so anyway (especially when delicious food is around). This recipe is courtesy of Judi Kopsack, Brooklyn's mother.

1 cup sugar
⅓ cup (a little over 5 tablespoons) butter, softened
2 eggs
3 to 4 ripe bananas, mashed
⅓ cup water
1⅔ cups brown-rice flour
1 teaspoon baking soda
¼ teaspoon baking powder
½ teaspoon salt
¾ cup blueberries

Preheat oven to 350°F. Line muffin pans with paper liners.

In a large mixing bowl, cream together sugar and butter, using a hand mixer. Stir in eggs. Add bananas and water, and mix for an additional 30 seconds. In a separate bowl, combine the brown-rice flour, baking soda, baking powder, and salt. Add the dry ingredients to the banana mixture, and mix by hand. Fold in the blueberries.

Pour the batter into the muffin pans, filling each two-thirds full. Bake 20 to 25 minutes until a toothpick inserted in the center of a muffin comes out clean. Cool slightly, then remove from pan and cool on a wire rack.

Makes 24 muffins

*A*pplesauce Bread with Teff Flour

Teff flour is soft and fine and works well in breads. This bread is particularly moist and dense. If you feel hesitant to try this grain, it may inspire you to know that my son, who is not the most adventurous eater, loves all things teff.

6 tablespoons butter, softened
½ cup sugar
1 egg, beaten
1 cup applesauce
1 cup teff flour
⅓ cup cornstarch
½ teaspoon baking soda
½ teaspoon cinnamon
Dash salt

Preheat oven to 350°F. Grease a loaf pan.

In a medium-size mixing bowl, cream together the butter and sugar. Add the egg, and mix together by hand. Stir in the applesauce. In a separate bowl, combine the flour, cornstarch, baking soda, cinnamon, and salt. Add the flour mixture to the applesauce mixture, and stir until combined.

Spoon batter into the greased loaf pan, and bake 50 minutes or until a toothpick inserted into the middle of the loaf comes out clean. Remove bread from pan, and allow to cool completely on a wire rack.

Makes 1 loaf

*A*maranth and Buckwheat Banana "Cake" Bread

According to my husband, this is the best banana bread he has ever tasted. It is very moist, dense, and cakelike.

6 tablespoons butter, softened
½ cup sugar
3 bananas, mashed
3 tablespoons 1 percent milk
½ cup buckwheat flour
½ cup amaranth flour
⅓ cup cornstarch
½ teaspoon baking soda

Preheat oven to 350°F. Grease a loaf pan.

In a large mixing bowl, cream together the butter and sugar by hand. Add the bananas and milk, stirring to combine. In a separate bowl, mix together the buckwheat flour, amaranth flour, cornstarch, and baking soda. Add the flour mixture to the banana mixture, stirring to combine.

Place batter in the greased loaf pan, and bake 50 minutes or until a toothpick inserted in the middle comes out clean. Remove bread from pan, and allow to cool completely on a wire rack.

Makes 1 loaf

*R*onni's Zucchini Cupcakes

This recipe is courtesy of Veronica Alicea, RD, a nutritionist specializing in celiac disease and a consultant to several producers of gluten-free foods, including Enjoy Life Foods and Heartland's Finest. The recipe calls for navy bean flour. Using bean flours in recipes is an easy way to increase your intake of fiber and iron.

3 eggs
2 cups granulated sugar
1 cup canola oil
1 teaspoon vanilla extract
2 cups grated raw zucchini
2½ cups navy bean flour
3 teaspoons cinnamon
1 teaspoon baking soda
1 teaspoon baking powder
1 teaspoon salt

Preheat oven to 350°F. Grease muffin pans or use cupcake liners.

In a large bowl, use a mixer to combine eggs, sugar, oil, and vanilla. Add zucchini and mix. In a separate bowl, sift together flour, cinnamon, baking soda, baking powder, and salt. Add flour mixture to wet mixture and mix well.

Fill prepared muffin pans two-thirds full. Bake 25 minutes or until cupcakes are golden brown.

Makes 24 cupcakes

Cynthia's Gluten-Free Cranberry Muffins

This recipe is courtesy of Cynthia Kupper, RD, a nutritionist and the executive director of the Gluten Intolerance Group of North America. Cynthia dedicates this recipe to Bette Hagman, a cookbook author known as the "Gluten-Free Gourmet" and one of the pioneers in gluten-free baking. The recipe calls for Bette's Gourmet Four Flour Blend (a flour blend developed by Bette Hagman) and Montina Pure Baking Supplement. The flour blend, which is a mixture of garfava flour, sorghum flour, cornstarch, and tapioca flour, can be ordered from Authentic Foods. Montina Pure Baking Supplement, which is a flour milled from the seed of Indian rice grass, can be ordered from Amazing Grains. For contact information, see Appendix A.

1 cup chopped raw cranberries
½ cup plus 2 tablespoons sugar
2 cups minus 2 tablespoons Bette's Gourmet Four Flour
   Blend
2 tablespoons Montina Pure Baking Supplement
2 teaspoons baking powder
½ teaspoon salt
1 teaspoon xanthan gum
1 egg
1 cup milk
¼ cup nonhydrogenated vegetable shortening, melted
1 small overripe banana, mashed
½ cup chopped nuts (optional)

Preheat oven to 400°F. Grease a muffin pan with 12 large or 16 medium cups.

Stir together the cranberries and ½ cup sugar. In a large mixing bowl, sift the flour blend, measure, and resift with Montina Pure, baking powder, salt, remaining 2 tablespoons sugar, and xanthan gum. In another mixing bowl, beat the egg, and then beat in the milk and melted shortening. Add the egg mixture all at once to the dry ingredients, and stir quickly until the flour is just dampened; the batter will not be smooth. With the last few stirs, fold in the cranberries, banana, and nuts, if desired.

Quickly spoon the batter into the muffin cups, filling each two-thirds full. Bake 20 to 25 minutes or until the muffin pulls away from the pan slightly. Serve hot.

Makes 12 large or 16 medium muffins

Connor's Gluten-Free Blueberry Muffins

This recipe is courtesy of Evelyn Tribole, M.S., RD, a nutritionist, author, and mother of a son with celiac disease. Visit Evelyn's website at evelyntribole.com. According to Evelyn's son Connor, these muffins are awesome and better than any store-bought muffin. This recipe uses a gluten-free baking mix, which is handy if you are just starting to experiment with gluten-free baking. Evelyn's preferred mix is Pamela's Baking and Pancake Mix, which is based on brown-rice flour, but you can substitute any gluten-free baking mix; just make sure that at least the first ingredient is a whole grain. This recipe also calls for flaxseed, a great source of fiber and heart-healthy omega-3 fatty acids. Flaxseed is carried in natural-foods stores, or you can order it from Bob's Red Mill and Arrowhead Mills (see Appendix A). Evelyn also recommends using eggs fortified with omega-3 fatty acids. These eggs should be available in your local supermarket.

> 1½ cups Pamela's Baking and Pancake Mix
> ⅔ cup sugar
> ¼ cup ground flaxseed (flax meal)
> ⅛ teaspoon cinnamon
> ¼ cup buttermilk
> ¼ cup canola oil
> 1 tablespoon vanilla
> 2 eggs (preferably fortified with omega-3 fatty acids)
> 1 cup fresh or frozen blueberries

Preheat oven to 350°F. Line a 12-cup muffin tin with foil baking cups, and lightly coat with gluten-free nonstick cooking spray.

In a medium-size bowl, combine the baking mix, sugar, flaxseed, and cinnamon. Add the buttermilk, oil, vanilla, and eggs. Mix by hand until thoroughly combined. Fold in the blueberries. Spoon batter into prepared muffin tins. Bake 20 to 22 minutes or until golden.

Makes 12 muffins

Elaine's Gluten-Free Corn Bread

This recipe is courtesy of Elaine Monarch, executive director of the Celiac Disease Foundation. This corn bread is absolutely delicious with chili.

2 cups whole-grain yellow cornmeal
2 teaspoons baking powder
1 teaspoon baking soda
Scant teaspoon salt
2 cups buttermilk
1 stick (½ cup) butter, melted and cooled
1 14¾-ounce can cream-style corn
2 cups shredded low-fat Monterey Jack cheese
2 cans (4 to 4½ ounces each) chopped mild green chilies
4 eggs, lightly beaten

Preheat oven to 350°F. Grease a 13″ × 9″ glass baking dish or metal baking pan.

Mix together by hand the cornmeal, baking powder, baking soda, and salt in a large bowl. Stir in the buttermilk, melted butter, corn, cheese, chilies, and eggs; mix until thoroughly blended.

Pour batter into prepared baking pan. Bake at least 1 hour or a little longer until top is browned and a toothpick inserted in the center comes out clean. Cool corn bread in the pan on a wire rack. The bread is excellent served slightly warm.

Makes one loaf (about 12 servings)

Andrew's Pumpkin Muffins

This recipe is courtesy of Jane Roberts, who together with her three children, Andrew, Emily, and Claire, has celiac disease. Thank you also to Jane's sister Carol Shilson, executive director of the University of Chicago Celiac Disease Center, for putting us in touch. This is the perfect fall muffin recipe!

⅔ cup nonhydrogenated vegetable shortening
2⅔ cups raw sugar
4 eggs
1 15-ounce can pumpkin
⅔ cup cold water
1⅓ cups millet flour
1 cup soy flour
1 cup tapioca starch
2 teaspoons baking soda
1½ teaspoons salt
½ teaspoon baking powder
2 to 3 tablespoons cinnamon (add more to taste)
¼ teaspoon ground cloves (optional)
¼ cup chopped nuts (optional)
¼ cup raisins (optional)

Preheat oven to 350°F. Use 2 muffin tins or loaf pans sprayed with gluten-free cooking spray.

Beat the shortening and sugar until fluffy. Stir in the eggs and pumpkin. Add the water and combine. Mix together the millet and soy flours, tapioca starch, baking soda, salt, baking powder, cinnamon, and cloves (if desired). Add to the pumpkin mixture and thoroughly combine. Mix in the nuts and raisins, if desired.

Pour the batter into muffin tins or loaf pans. Bake 70 minutes. Muffins are done when a toothpick inserted in the center comes out clean. Muffins can cool in pans or on rack.

Makes 24 muffins or 2 loaves

Savory Millet Bread

This bread has the crumbly texture of a southern corn bread. Try serving it with chili—delicious!

1½ cups millet flour
¼ cup cornstarch
¼ teaspoon baking powder
½ teaspoon baking soda
½ teaspoon salt
1 teaspoon garlic powder
1 teaspoon dried cilantro
1 cup milk
1 cup grated low-fat cheddar cheese
1 egg, beaten
6 tablespoons butter, melted and cooled

Preheat oven to 350° F. Lightly grease a 9-inch square baking pan.

In a medium-size mixing bowl, use a fork to combine the millet flour, cornstarch, baking powder, baking soda, salt, garlic powder, and cilantro. Add the milk, cheese, egg, and cooled butter. Stir just until combined.

Pour the batter into the prepared pan. Bake 25 to 30 minutes until the top is slightly browned and a toothpick inserted in the center comes out clean. Allow to cool completely on a wire rack before cutting and removing from pan.

Makes one 9-inch square loaf (about nine 3" × 3" servings)

Desserts

Anne's Yummy Gluten-Free Chocolate Chip Cookie Bars

This recipe, adapted from Nestlé's Toll House cookie recipe, is courtesy of Anne Lee, M.S. Ed., RD, a nutritionist at the Celiac Disease Center at Columbia University. If you are starting to eat oats again, this is the perfect recipe for you.

> 1¾ cups chick-pea flour (also known as garbanzo bean flour)
> 1 cup gluten-free oats
> 1 teaspoon baking soda
> 1 teaspoon salt
> ½ cup (1 stick) butter
> ½ cup peanut butter
> ¾ cup granulated sugar
> ¾ cup packed brown sugar
> 1 teaspoon vanilla
> 2 eggs
> 2 cups chocolate chips

Preheat oven to 375°F. Grease a 9″ × 13″ baking pan.

In a medium-size bowl, combine the chick-pea flour, oats, baking soda, and salt. In a large mixing bowl, cream together the butter, peanut butter, granulated and brown sugars, and vanilla. Add the eggs one at a time, beating after each addition. Gradually add the flour mixture to the egg mixture. Stir in the chocolate chips.

Spoon dough into the prepared pan. Bake 20 to 25 minutes until golden brown. Cool and cut into bars.

Makes 24 bars

Grandma's Indian Pudding

Desserts sometimes can be the trickiest part of the meal for persons with celiac disease. Indian pudding is a traditional dessert that just happens to be made without gluten-containing ingredients. This recipe was passed down from my grandmother, Betty Hatch. Serve this dessert with a little vanilla ice cream on a cold winter's day. It is sure to be a hit!

4 cups 1 percent milk
4 tablespoons whole-grain cornmeal
⅓ cup molasses
1 egg, well beaten
1 tablespoon butter
⅓ cup sugar
½ teaspoon ground ginger
½ teaspoon ground cinnamon
¼ teaspoon salt

Preheat oven to 300°F. Grease a 1½-quart baking dish.

Scald 3 cups milk. Combine cornmeal and molasses, and stir into scalded milk. Cook mixture for 4 minutes at a slow boil, stirring constantly. Remove mixture from heat, and stir in the egg, butter, sugar, ginger, cinnamon, and salt. Pour mixture into the greased baking dish, and bake 30 minutes. Pour the remaining 1 cup milk over the pudding, and continue to bake for an additional 2 hours. Serve warm.

Makes 6 servings

Nancy's Fruit Bars

This recipe is courtesy of Nancy Patin Falini, M.A., RD, LDN, a nutritionist and the author of Gluten-Free Friends: An Activity Book for Kids. *These bars are absolutely delicious and much tastier and heartier than the gluten-containing variety made with whole wheat flour and oats. The quinoa flakes add a crunchy, nutty texture and flavor that is especially nice for those unable to eat nuts in addition to gluten.*

> 2 cups garbanzo bean flour (also known as chick-pea flour)
> ⅓ cup quinoa flakes
> ½ cup oil (any kind)
> ¼ cup honey
> 1 egg or ¼ cup egg substitute
> 1 tablespoon vanilla
> 1 cup fruit spread, jam, or jelly (for topping)

Preheat oven to 350°F. Grease a 13″ × 9″ baking pan.

Mix together the flour, quinoa flakes, oil, honey, egg, and vanilla until the dough looks grainy. Press the dough into the greased pan. Spread the fruit topping over the dough. If using egg substitute, Nancy recommends mixing 1 tablespoon ground flax and 3 tablespoons warm water. Allow to set 5–15 minutes before using.

Bake 25 to 30 minutes or until a toothpick inserted in the center comes out clean. Let cool on a wire rack. Cut into 2¼″ × 2⅛″ bars, and remove from pan.

Makes 24 bars

*P*eanut Butter Shortbread with Teff Flour

This recipe calls for teff flour. Teff is grown in the United States in Idaho.

1¼ cups ivory teff flour
2 tablespoons cornstarch
¾ cup natural peanut butter (smooth only)
4 tablespoons butter, softened
½ cup sugar

Preheat oven to 300°F. In a small mixing bowl, combine the flour and cornstarch. In a medium-size mixing bowl, thoroughly combine the peanut butter and butter. (It is very important that you use only smooth peanut butter, because chunky style will cause the shortbread to crumble.) Add the sugar, combining well. Slowly add the flour, mixing by hand.

Spread the mixture in a 9-inch square baking pan, patting it down by hand. Bake 45 minutes. Place the pan on a wire rack, and allow the shortbread to completely cool in the pan. Cut into 1½" × 3" bars, and use a narrow spatula to remove from pan.

Makes 18 bars

Evelyn's Macadamia Nut–Chocolate Chip Cookies

This recipe is courtesy of Evelyn Tribole, M.S., RD, a nutritionist, author, and mother of a son with celiac disease. Visit Evelyn's website at evelyntribole.com. This recipe uses a gluten-free baking mix, which is handy if you are just starting to experiment with gluten-free baking. Evelyn's preferred mix is Pamela's Baking and Pancake Mix, which is based on brown rice, but you can substitute any gluten-free baking mix; just make sure that at least the first ingredient is a whole grain. This recipe also calls for flaxseed, a great source of fiber and heart-healthy omega-3 fatty acids. Evelyn also recommends using eggs fortified with omega-3 fatty acids, available in your local supermarket.

½ cup canola oil
2 eggs (preferably fortified with omega-3 fatty acids)
¼ cup granulated sugar
¼ cup brown sugar
1 tablespoon vanilla
1½ cups Pamela's Baking and Pancake Mix
⅓ cup ground flaxseed (flax meal)
½ cup mini chocolate chips
⅔ cup macadamia nut halves

Preheat oven to 350°F. Lightly coat two baking sheets with gluten-free nonstick cooking spray.

In a medium bowl, mix together the oil, eggs, granulated and brown sugars, and vanilla until thoroughly combined. Stir in the baking mix and flaxseed until thoroughly combined. Stir in the chocolate chips.

Spoon the dough by tablespoonfuls onto the prepared baking sheets. Place about 3 macadamia halves on top of each cookie. Bake until golden, about 11 minutes. Cool about 5 minutes, and transfer cookies from the baking sheets to a plate.

Makes 2 dozen cookies

Mary's Chocolate-Caramel Bars

This recipe is courtesy of Mary Schluckebier, M.A., a home economist and the executive director of the Celiac Sprue Association. These bars are absolutely decadent! The recipe calls for brown-rice syrup. Gluten-free brown-rice syrup is available from Lundberg Family Farms (see Appendix A).

CRUST
1 cup navy bean flour
¼ cup brown sugar
¼ teaspoon salt
½ cup (1 stick) chilled unsalted butter, cut into ½-inch cubes
2 tablespoons ice-cold water
1 egg yolk

LAYER 1
1 14-ounce can sweetened condensed milk
½ cup brown sugar
6 tablespoons (¾ stick) butter, diced
2 tablespoons gluten-free brown-rice syrup
1 teaspoon lemon juice
2 to 4 tablespoons chopped pecans
2 teaspoons vanilla

LAYER 2
6 ounces bittersweet or semisweet chocolate
3 tablespoons whipping cream
2 to 4 tablespoons finely chopped pecans

For crust: Preheat oven to 350°F. Line an 11″ × 7″ × 2″ baking pan with parchment paper, or lightly butter the pan. Mix the flour, brown sugar, and salt in a food processor. Add the cold butter, and process until a coarse meal forms. Add cold water and egg yolk. Process until clumps form. Press the dough into the bottom of the pan. Bake until golden brown, about 20 minutes. Cool completely.

Layer 1: Whisk all ingredients in a medium saucepan over medium heat until the sugar dissolves, butter melts, and mixture boils. Boil gently, whisking constantly, until the caramel reaches soft-ball stage or temperature registers 225°F on a candy thermometer. Pour the caramel evenly over the crust; cool to set.

Layer 2: Slowly melt the chocolate with the cream in a microwave on high for 1 minute, stirring until melted, checking at 30-second intervals, or in a double boiler on the stovetop, stirring occasionally. Spread the chocolate over the warm but set caramel; sprinkle with the nuts. Refrigerate until chocolate is set, approximately 15–30 minutes. Cut into 1-inch squares. Cover and keep refrigerated until 30 minutes before serving.

Makes about 6 dozen 1-inch square bars

Appendix A
Resources

Celiac Disease Support Groups

Celiac Disease Foundation (CDF)
13251 Ventura Blvd., Suite 1
Studio City, CA 91604
Phone: 818-990-2354
Fax: 818-990-2379
Website: celiac.org
E-mail: cdf@celiac.org

Celiac Sprue Association (CSA)
P.O. Box 31700
Omaha, NE 68131
Phone: 402-558-0600
Phone (toll-free): 877-272-4272
Fax: 402-558-1347
Website: csaceliacs.org
E-mail: celiacs@csaceliacs.org

The Gluten Intolerance Group (GIG)
31214 124th Ave., SE
Auburn, WA 98092
Phone: 253-833-6655
Fax: 253-833-6675
Website: gluten.net
E-mail: info@gluten.net

Canadian Celiac Association
5170 Dixie Rd., Suite 204
Mississauga, ON, Canada L4W 1E3
Phone: 800-363-7296
Fax: 905-363-7296
Website: celiac.ca
E-mail: info@celiac.ca

Celiac Disease Medical Centers

Beth Israel Deaconess Medical Center Celiac Center
Beth Israel Deaconess Medical Center
Nutrition Services, Rabb B06
330 Brookline Ave.
Boston, MA 02215
Phone: 617-667-2135
Website: http://bidmc.harvard.edu/display
    .asp?node_id=5449
Dietitian: Melinda Dennis, M.S., RD

Celiac Disease Center at Columbia University
Harkness Pavilion
180 Fort Washington Ave., Suite 934
New York, NY 10032
Phone: 212-342-4529

Website: celiacdiseasecenter.columbia.edu
Dietitian: Anne Lee, M.S. Ed., RD

University of Chicago Celiac Disease Program
The University of Chicago Medical Center
5839 S. Maryland Ave., MC4069
Chicago, IL 60637
Phone: 773-702-3051
Website: uchospitals.edu/specialties/celiac

**University of Maryland School of Medicine Center
   for Celiac Research**
20 Penn St., Room S303B
Baltimore, MD 21201
Phone: 410-328-6749 or 800-492-5538
Website: celiaccenter.org
Dietitian: Pamela Cureton, RD

**Wm. K. Warren Medical Research Center for
   Celiac Disease**
9500 Gilman Dr.
La Jolla, CA 92093-0623
Phone: 858-822-1022
Website: http://celiaccenter.ucsd.edu
Dietitian: Susan Algert, Ph.D., RD

Books

Gluten-Free Cookbooks

Carlyle-Gauthier, Rachel, and Billie McCrea. *Gluten-Free Mama's Best Baking Recipes.* Longwood, FL: Xulon Press, 2007.
Fenster, Carol. *Gluten-Free Quick and Easy: From Prep to Plate Without the Fuss.* New York: Avery, 2007.

Hagman, Bette. *The Gluten-Free Gourmet Cooks Comfort Foods: Creating Old Favorites with the New Flours.* New York: Henry Holt & Co., Owl Books, 2005.

———. *The Gluten-Free Gourmet Cooks Fast and Healthy: Wheat-Free Recipes with Less Fuss and Less Fat.* New York: Henry Holt & Co., Owl Books, 2000.

Sarros, Connie. *Wheat-Free, Gluten-Free Reduced-Calorie Cookbook.* New York: McGraw-Hill, 2004.

Shepard, Jules E. D. *Nearly Normal Cooking for Gluten-Free Eating: A Fresh Approach to Cooking and Living Without Wheat and Gluten.* Charleston, SC: BookSurge Publishing, 2006.

Washburn, Donna, and Heather Butt. *The Best Gluten-Free Family Cookbook.* Toronto: Robert Rose, 2005.

———. *Complete Gluten-Free Cookbook: 150 Gluten-Free, Lactose-Free Recipes, Many with Egg-Free Variations.* Toronto: Robert Rose, 2007.

General Information on Celiac Disease and the Gluten-Free Diet

Case, Shelley. *Gluten-Free Diet: A Comprehensive Resource Guide*, rev. ed. Regina, SK Canada: Case Nutrition Consulting, 2006.

Green, Peter H. R., and Rory Jones. *Celiac Disease: A Hidden Epidemic.* New York: HarperCollins, 2006.

Korn, Danna. *Wheat-Free, Worry-Free: The Art of Happy, Healthy Gluten-Free Living.* Carlsbad, CA: Hay House, 2002.

Lowell, Jax Peters. *The Gluten-Free Bible: The Thoroughly Indispensable Guide to Negotiating Life Without Wheat.* New York: Henry Holt & Co., Owl Books, 2005.

Eating Away from Home and the Gluten-Free Diet

The Essential Restaurant Guide. Arlington, VA: Triumph Dining, 2007.

Koeller, Kim, and Robert La France. *Let's Eat Out! Your Passport to Living Gluten and Allergy Free.* Chicago: R & R Publishing, 2005.

Ries, LynnRae. *Waiter, Is There Wheat in My Soup? The Official Guide to Dining Out, Shopping, and Traveling Gluten-Free and Allergen-Free.* Phoenix, AZ: What No Wheat Publishing, 2005.

Children and Celiac Disease

Falini, Nancy P. *Gluten-Free Friends: An Activity Book for Kids.* Centennial, CO: Savory Palate, Inc., 2003.

Korn, Danna. *Kids with Celiac Disease: A Family Guide to Raising Happy, Healthy, Gluten-Free Children.* Bethesda, MD: Woodbine House, 2001.

Kruszka, Bonnie J. *Eating Gluten-Free with Emily: A Story for Children with Celiac Disease.* Bethesda, MD: Woodbine House, 2005.

Gluten-Free Medications and Supplements

Milazzo, Marcia. *Celiac Disease: A Guide Through the Medicine Cabinet,* 2006, available at www.celiacmeds.com.

———— . *The Directory of Drug Manufacturers,* available at www.celiacmeds.com.

Magazines

Gluten-Free Living
Quarterly magazine for people with celiac disease and dermatitis herpetiformis.
Ann Whelan, Editor/Publisher
560 Warburton Ave., 2nd floor
Hastings-on-Hudson, NY 10706
Phone: 914-231-6361
Website: glutenfreeliving.com
E-mail: info@glutenfreeliving.com

Sully's Living Without
Quarterly magazine for people with food allergies,
   intolerances, and sensitivities, including celiac disease.
Peggy A. Wagener, President/Publisher
P.O. Box 2126
Northbrook, IL 60065
Phone: 847-480-8810
Website: livingwithout.com
E-mail: Editor@LivingWithout.com

Celiac Disease and Religious Issues

Low-Gluten Altar Bread

Benedictine Sisters of Perpetual Adoration
Benedictine Monastery
Altar Breads Department
31970 State Hwy. P
Clyde, MO 64432
Phone: 800-223-2772 (Altar Bread Department)
Website: benedictinesisters.org
Manufactures low-gluten altar breads.

Gluten-Free Altar Bread

Ener-G Foods, Inc.
5960 First Ave. S
P.O. Box 84487
Seattle, WA 98124-5787
Phone: 800-331-5222
Website: ener-g.com
Manufactures gluten-free rice-based altar breads.

Oat Matzos

Shemura Oat Matzos
Rabbi E. Kestenbaum, Producer
22 Eagle Lodge
Golders Green
London NW 11 8BD England
Phone: +44 208 455 9476
Website: glutenfreeoatmatzos.com
Manufactures oat-based matzo.

Manufacturers of Gluten-Free Foods

Adrienne's Gourmet Food
849 Ward Dr.
Santa Barbara, CA 93111
Phone: 805-964-6848
Website: adriennes.com

Amazing Grains
P.O. Box 919
Pablo, MT 59855
Phone: 406-675-3536
Phone (toll-free): 877-278-6585
Website: amazinggrains.com

Arrowhead Mills
The Hain Celestial Group
4600 Sleepytime Dr.
Boulder, CO 80301
Phone: 800-434-4246
Website: arrowheadmills.com

Authentic Foods
1850 W. 169th St., Suite B
Gardena, CA 90247
Phone: 310-366-7612 or 800-806-4737
Website: authenticfoods.com

Barbara's Bakery, Inc.
3900 Cypress Dr.
Petaluma, CA 94954
Phone: 866-972-6879
Website: barbarasbakery.com

The Birkett Mills
(Pocono brand)
163 Main St.
Penn Yan, NY 14527
Phone: 315-536-3311
Website: thebirkettmills.com

Bob's Red Mill
5209 SE International Way
Milwaukie, OR 97222
Phone: 800-349-2173
Website: bobsredmill.com

Cream Hill Estates, Ltd.
9633 rue Clement
La Salle, QC, Canada H8R 4B4
Phone: 866-727-3628
Website: pure-oats.com

Eden Foods
701 Tecumseh Rd.
Clinton, MI 49236

Phone: 888-424-3336
Website: edenfoods.com

Ener-G Foods, Inc.
5960 First Ave. S
P.O. Box 84487
Seattle, WA 98124-5787
Phone: 800-331-5222
Website: ener-g.com

Enjoy Life Foods
3810 River Rd.
Schiller Park, IL 60176
Phone: 847-260-0300
Website: enjoylifefoods.com

Food Directions, Inc.
(Tinkyada brand)
120 Melford Dr., Unit 8
Scarborough, ON, Canada M1B 2X5
Phone: 416-609-0016
Website: tinkyada.com

Genisoy Food Company
100 W. 5th St., Suite 700
Tulsa, OK 74103
Phone: 866-606-3829
Website: genisoy.com

Gibb's Wild Rice
P.O. Box 277
Deer River, MN 56636
Phone: 800-344-6378
Website: gibbswildrice.com

Gifts of Nature, Inc.
810 7th St. E, #17
Polson, MT 59860
Phone: 888-275-0003
Website: giftsofnature.net

Gluten Free Oats
578 Lane 9
Powell, WY 82435
Phone: 307-754-2058
Website: glutenfreeoats.com

Gluten-Free Pantry
P.O. Box 840
Glastonbury, CT 06033
Phone: 860-633-3826
Website: glutenfree.com

Glutino Food Group
2055 Boul. Dagenais Quest
Laval, QC, Canada H7L 5V1
Phone: 800-363-3438
Website: glutino.com

Heartland's Finest
24291 Veterans Memorial Hwy.
Hillman, MI 49746
Phone: 888-658-8909
Website: heartlandsfinest.com

Kinnikinnick Foods, Inc.
10940-120 St. (store location)
Edmonton, AB, Canada T5H 3P7
Phone: 877-503-4466
Website:kinnikinnick.com

Lundberg Family Farms
5370 Church St.
P.O. Box 369
Richvale, CA 95974-0369
Phone: 530-882-4551
Website: lundberg.com

Maple Grove Food and Beverage
(Pastariso, Pastato, Café Bonjour, and Macariz brands)
8175 Winston Churchill Blvd.
Norval, ON, Canada L0P 1K0
Phone: 905-451-7423
Website: maplegrovefoods.com

Nature's Path Foods, Inc.
(Lifestream, Nature's Path, and Envirokidz brands)
9100 Van Horne Way
Richmond, BC, Canada V6X 1W3
Phone: 888-808-9505
Website: naturespath.com

Northern Quinoa Corporation
P.O. Box 519
428 3rd St.
Kamsack, SK, Canada S0A 1S0
Phone: 306-542-3949 or 866-368-9304
Website: quinoa.com

Nu-World Amaranth, Inc.
P.O. Box 2202
Naperville, IL 60567
Phone: 630-369-6819
Website: nuworldamaranth.com

Only Oats
316 1st Ave. E
Regina, SK, Canada, S4N 5H2
Phone: 866-461-3663
Website: onlyoats.com

Pamela's Products
200 Clara Ave.
Ukiah, CA 95482
Phone: 707-462-6605
Website: pamelasproducts.com

Perky's (manufactured for Enjoy Life Natural Foods)
3810 River Rd.
Schiller Park, IL 60176
Phone: 888-473-7597
Website: perkysnaturalfoods.com

Quinoa Corporation
(Ancient Harvest brand)
P.O. Box 279
222 E. Redondo Beach Blvd., Unit B
Gardena, CA 90248
Phone: 310-217-8125
Website: quinoa.net

Shiloh Farms
Website: shilohfarms.net

Sylvan Border Farm
P.O. Box 277
Willits, CA 95490-0277
Phone: 800-297-5399
Website: sylvanborderfarm.com

The Teff Company
Phone: 888-822-2221
Website: teffco.com

Twin Valley Mills, LLC
R.R. 1, Box 45
Ruskin, NE 68974
Phone: 402-279-3965
Website: twinvalleymills.com

U.S. Mills, Inc.
(Erewhon and New Morning brands)
200 Reservoir St.
Needham, MA 02494-3146
Phone: 781-444-0440
Website: usmillsinc.com

Van's International Foods
3285 E. Vernon Ave.
Vernon, CA 90058
Phone: 323-585-5581
Website: vansintl.com

Manufacturers of Gluten-Free Beers

Anheuser Busch (Redbridge beer)
St. Louis, MO
Website: redbridgebeer.com
Anheuser-Busch manufactures Redbridge beer, made from sorghum. Visit the brand's website for more information, including a locator service for finding retailers by zip code.

Bard's Tale Beer (Dragon's Gold beer)
Phone: 816-524-3270
Website: bardsbeer.com
Bard's Tale Beer manufactures Dragon's Gold beer, made from sorghum. Visit the company's website for more information, including a state-by-state listing of retailers and restaurants where this beer can be found.

Lakefront Brewery (New Grist beer)
Phone: 414-372-8800
Website: newgrist.com
Lakefront Brewery manufactures New Grist beer from sorghum and rice. Visit the company website for more information, including how to order online.

Ramapo Valley Brewers (Honey Lager)
Phone: 866-932-5918
Website: ramapovalleybrewery.com
Ramapo Valley Brewers manufactures Passover Honey Lager. Visit the company's website for more information, including a retail locator service and directions for ordering online.

Manufacturers of Gluten-Free Supplements

Freeda Vitamins, Inc.
47-25 34th St., 3rd floor
Long Island City, NY 11101
Phone: 800-777-3737
Website: freedavitamins.com

Nature Made
P.O. Box 9606
Mission Hills, CA 91346
Phone: 800-276-2878
Website: naturemade.com

Pioneer Nutritional Formulas
304 Shelburne Center Rd.
Shelburne Falls, MA 01370
Phone: 800-458-8483
Website: pioneernutritional.com

Websites

General Information on Celiac Disease

The Celiac Disease Awareness Campaign of the National Institutes of Health (http://celiac.nih.gov)
Celiac disease information from the National Digestive Diseases Information Clearinghouse (http://digestive.niddk.nih.gov/ddiseases/pubs/celiac)
National Institutes of Health Consensus Development Conference Statement on Celiac Disease (http://consensus.nih.gov/2004/2004CeliacDisease118html.htm)

Celiac Disease and Osteoporosis

"What People with Celiac Disease Need to Know About Osteoporosis." Information on celiac disease and osteoporosis is provided at this website of the National Institute of Arthritis and Musculoskeletal and Skin Diseases, National Institutes of Health, Department of Health and Human Services (niams.nih.gov/Health_Info/Bone/Osteoporosis/conditions_Behaviors/celiac.asp)

Lactose Intolerance

General information on lactose intolerance is provided at
this website of the National Digestive Diseases Information
Center Clearinghouse (digestive.niddk.nih.gov/ddiseases/
pub/lactoseintolerance)

Food Labeling

The complete Food Allergen Labeling and Consumer Protection
Act of 2004 is provided at this website of the U.S. Food and
Drug Administration, Center for Food Safety and Applied
Nutrition (www.cfsan.fda.gov/~dms/alrgact.html)
The online publication "Advice to Consumers: Food Allergen
Labeling and Consumer Protection Act of 2004 Questions
and Answers" is available at this website of the U.S. Food and
Drug Administration, Center for Food Safety and Applied
Nutrition (www. cfsan.fda.gov/~dms/alrgqa.html)
The FDA's complete proposed rule for use of the term *gluten-free*
on food labels (www. cfsan.fda.gov/~lrd/fr070123.html)
Health Canada's position on the safety of oats (hc-sc.gc
.ca/fn-an/securit/allerg/cel-coe/oats_cd-avoine_e.html)

General Nutrition

The USDA National Nutrient Database for Standard Reference
(nal.usda.gov/fnic/foodcomp/search)
The *Dietary Guidelines for Americans, 2005* (health.gov/
dietaryguidelines/dga2005/document)
My Pyramid Plan (mypyramid.gov)

Alcohol Manufacture and Labeling

Contains an excellent article on how sake is made (sake-world
.com)
Online encyclopedia with articles on brewing, distillation, and
alcoholic beverages (http://en.wikipedia.org)
The Bureau of Alcohol, Tobacco, Firearms, and Explosives website, containing information on the labeling of alcoholic beverages. In the search engine, type *alcohol labeling* (atf.treas
.gov/cgi-bin/atfgovsearch.cgi)

Religious Issues

Online article about wheat-starch-based low-gluten Communion
wafers (conceptionabbey.org/TowerTopics/TTSummer04/
Sisters.htm). Click on "Magazine" and then "Summer 2004,"
scroll down to article titled, "Sisters' discovery answers a host
of prayers."

Medications

An excellent article by pharmacist Steven Plogsted entitled,
"Medications and Celiac Disease—Tips from a Pharmacist."
Free online access to this article is available (healthsystem
.virginia.edu/internet/digestive-health/nutritionarticles/
PlogstedArticle.pdf)

Appendix B
Reading Food Labels

Sample Food Label

Manufacturers of food products must declare on their labels the presence of an ingredient that is or contains protein from any of the eight major food allergens: milk, eggs, fish, crustacean shellfish, tree nuts, peanuts, wheat, and soybeans. They have two options for doing this: allergens may either be declared in the ingredient list or be identified in a separate Contains statement immediately following the ingredient list. The following examples show each option:

❖ **Ingredients:** Enriched flour (**wheat** flour, malted barley, niacin, reduced iron, thiamin mononitrate, riboflavin, folic acid), sugar, partially hydrogenated soybean oil, and/or cottonseed oil, high fructose corn syrup, whey (**milk**), **eggs**, vanilla, natural and artificial flavoring, salt, leavening (sodium acid pyrophosphate, monocalcium phosphate), lecithin (**soy**), mono- and diglycerides (emulsifier)

❖ Contains Wheat, Milk, Egg, and Soy

Source: U.S. Food and Drug Administration, Center for Food Safety and Applied Nutrition, "Advice to Consumers: Food

Allergen Labeling and Consumer Protection Act of 2004 Questions and Answers," December 12, 2005; updated July 18, 2006. Available at www.cfsan.fda.gov/~dms/alrgqa.html, accessed June 5, 2007.

Nutrition Facts Label

Nutrition Facts

Serving Size 1 cup (228g)
Servings Per Container 2

Amount Per Serving

Calories 250	Calories from Fat 110

% Daily Value*

Total Fat 12g	18%
Saturated Fat 3g	15%
Trans Fat 3g	
Cholesterol 30mg	10%
Sodium 470mg	20%
Total Carbohydrate 31g	10%
Dietary Fiber 0g	0%
Sugars 5g	
Protein 5g	

Vitamin A	4%
Vitamin C	2%
Calcium	20%
Iron	4%

* Percent Daily Values are based on a 2,000 calorie diet. Your Daily Values may be higher or lower depending on your calorie needs:

	Calories:	2,000	2,500
Total Fat	Less than	65g	80g
Sat Fat	Less than	20g	25g
Cholesterol	Less than	300mg	300mg
Sodium	Less than	2,400mg	2,400mg
Total Carbohydrate		300g	375g
Dietary Fiber		25g	30g

Source: Food and Drug Administration, "How to Understand and Use the Nutrition Facts Label," www.cfsan.fda
.gov/~dms/label-dl.html.

Use the Nutrition Facts Label to Help You

* ❖ Make product comparisons, being careful to compare products with similar serving sizes.
* ❖ Choose products that contain 0 grams of trans fat.
* ❖ Choose products low in saturated fat: those with a % Daily Value of 5 percent or less.
* ❖ Choose products that are good sources of fiber: those with a % Daily Value of 20 percent or more.
* ❖ Choose products that are good sources of calcium: those with a % Daily Value of 20 percent or more.
* ❖ Choose products that are good sources of iron: those with a % Daily Value of 20 percent or more.

For more information on using the Nutrition Facts label, see the Food and Drug Administration's online publication "How to Understand and Use the Nutrition Facts Label," available at www.cfsan.fda.gov/~dms/foodlab.html.

Ingredient Information

Caramel (21 CFR 73.85)

According to the Code of Federal Regulations (CFR), a compilation of government rules, caramel is a color additive made from heating any of the following carbohydrates: dextrose, invert sugar, lactose, malt syrup, molasses, starch hydrolysates, or sucrose.

* For FDA-regulated foods, if caramel used in a food product contains protein derived from wheat, the word *wheat* must be stated on the food label.
* According to the website of caramel color manufacturer DD Williamson, cornstarch hydrolysate is used most often by manufacturers of caramel color. (This information is available at caramel.com/a-156-297-The-Basics-of-Caramel Colors.aspx.)
* For FDA-regulated foods, caramel could be derived from malt syrup (barley), and this might not be stated on the food label. *Remember, however, that caramel is probably derived from corn.*
* For USDA-regulated foods (meat products, poultry products, and egg products), caramel used in a food product could be derived from barley or wheat, and this might not be stated on the food label. *Remember, however, that caramel is probably derived from corn.*
* Bottom line: Caramel in both FDA and USDA-regulated foods is most likely gluten free.

Dextrin (21 CFR 184.1277)

According to the CFR, dextrin is a starch made from heating any of the following starches: corn, waxy maize, waxy milo, potato, arrowroot, wheat, rice, tapioca, or sage.

* For FDA-regulated foods, if dextrin used in a food product contains protein derived from wheat, the word *wheat* must be stated on the food label.
* For USDA-regulated foods, dextrin could contain protein derived from wheat, and this might not be stated on the food label.

❖ Bottom line: If you don't see the word *wheat* on the label of an FDA-regulated food product containing dextrin, the dextrin does not contain wheat protein. Dextrin in a USDA-regulated product could contain protein derived from wheat.

Glucose Syrup (21 CFR 168.120)

According to the CFR, glucose syrup is a nutritive sweetener made from edible starch.

❖ For FDA-regulated foods, if glucose syrup used in a food product contains protein derived from wheat, the word *wheat* must be stated on the food label.

❖ For USDA-regulated foods, glucose syrup could contain protein derived from wheat, and this might not be stated on the food label.

❖ Bottom line: If you don't see the word *wheat* on the label of an FDA-regulated product containing glucose syrup, the glucose syrup does not contain wheat protein. Glucose syrup in a USDA-regulated product could contain protein derived from wheat.

Malt (21 CFR 184.1443.a)

According to the CFR, malt is a liquid or powder made from *barley* grain that has been softened and allowed to germinate (sprout).

❖ Bottom line: Do not eat foods containing malt (unless the label states that a gluten-free grain was used to make the malt).

Malt Syrup/Malt Extract (21 CFR 184.1445)

According to the CFR, malt syrup or malt extract is a sweet, sticky liquid made from germinated *barley* grain (malt). It is generally used as a flavoring in food.

❖ Bottom line: Do not eat foods containing malt syrup or malt extract.

Maltodextrin (21 CFR 184.1444)

According to the CFR, maltodextrin is a starch made from corn, potato, or rice. According to the FDA, other starches, including wheat, may be used by manufacturers as long as they are generally recognized as safe.

❖ For FDA-regulated foods, if maltodextrin used in a food product contains protein from wheat, the word *wheat* must be stated on the food label.
❖ For USDA-regulated foods, maltodextrin could contain protein derived from wheat, and this might not be stated on the food label.
❖ Bottom line: If you don't see the word *wheat* on the label of an FDA-regulated food product containing maltodextrin, the maltodextrin does not contain wheat protein. Maltodextrin in a USDA-regulated product could contain protein derived from wheat.

Modified Food Starch (21 CFR 172.892)

Modified food starch is starch that has been altered through treatment with heat, acid, or enzymes. The CFR specifies what can be used to modify starch but not what starches may be modified. Therefore, modified food starch may be made from wheat.

- ❖ For FDA-regulated foods, if a modified food starch used in a food product contains protein derived from wheat, the word *wheat* must be stated on the food label.
- ❖ For USDA-regulated foods, modified food starch could contain protein derived from wheat, and this might not be stated on the food label.
- ❖ Bottom line: If you don't see the word *wheat* on the label of an FDA-regulated product containing modified food starch, the modified food starch does not contain wheat protein. Modified food starch in a USDA-regulated product could contain protein derived from wheat.

Natural Flavoring (21 CFR 101.22)

According to the CFR, natural flavorings may be made from a variety of sources, including wheat, barley, and rye.

- ❖ For FDA-regulated foods, if a natural flavoring contains protein derived from wheat, the word *wheat* must be stated on the food label.
- ❖ For FDA-regulated foods, natural flavoring could be derived from barley, but if so, it will most likely be listed as malt flavoring on the food label.
- ❖ For FDA-regulated foods, natural flavoring could be derived from rye. Products with rye flavoring are likely to be bread products that you wouldn't eat anyway.
- ❖ For USDA-regulated foods, if a natural flavor contains wheat, barley, or rye proteins, these ingredients will be stated on the food label by their common or usual names.
- ❖ Bottom line: If you don't see the words *wheat, barley, rye,* or *malt* on the label of a product containing natural flavor, the natural flavor most likely does not contain protein derived from these sources.

Protein Hydrolysates (21 CFR 101.22) (21 CFR 102.22)

According to the CFR, the protein source of a protein hydroly-sate, such as hydrolyzed vegetable protein (HVP) or hydrolyzed plant protein (HPP), must be declared on the food label (for example, hydrolyzed wheat protein). In addition, according to the CFR, protein hydrolysates may not be included under the term *natural flavor* on the food label.

* Bottom line: Do not eat foods containing hydrolyzed wheat protein.

Seasoning (CPG 7109.18)

The Compliance Policy Guide (CPG), an explanation of govern-ment regulations, states that individual spices, flavorings, and coloring ingredients must be named on a food label only in cases of articles sold as spices, flavorings, or colorings. In other words, if you were to buy a food coloring, the ingredients would have to be listed. But if the food coloring is an ingredient in another food, the specific colorings do not have to be named. In the case of a seasoning mix, spices, colorings, and flavorings may be declared collectively; ingredients other than spices, colorings or flavoring ingredients may not.

* For an FDA-regulated food, if a seasoning mix contains any ingredients containing wheat protein, the word *wheat* would be stated on the food label. This means that if a flavoring in the seasoning mix contains protein derived from wheat, the word *wheat* must be stated on the food label.
* For an FDA-regulated food, if a seasoning mix contains a fla-voring, the flavoring could be derived from barley, but if so, it will most likely be listed as malt flavoring on the food label.

* For a USDA-regulated food, if a seasoning mix contains a flavoring that contains protein from wheat, barley, or rye, these ingredients would be listed on the food label by their common or usual names.
* Bottom line: If you don't see the words *wheat, barley, rye,* or *malt* on the label of a food product containing seasonings, the seasoning most likely does not contain protein derived from these sources.

Starch (CPG 7104.01)

According to the Compliance Policy Guide, when the word *starch* is used on a food label, it means corn. If another source is used, it should be labeled.

* Bottom line: If the word *wheat* is not included on the label of a product containing starch, the starch does not contain wheat protein.

Important Note About Ingredients in USDA-Regulated Foods

Keep in mind that the Food Safety and Inspection Service of the USDA encourages manufacturers to list food allergens on product labels. Currently, however, only the common or usual name of ingredients must be included. Common or usual names of ingredients include *flour, maltodextrin, caramel,* and so forth. However, the Food Safety and Inspection Service of the USDA is in the process of developing regulations for the labeling of food allergens.

Important Note About Labeling of Wheat-Based Ingredients in FDA-Regulated Foods

Under FALCPA, if an ingredient in an FDA-regulated food product contains protein from wheat, the word *wheat* must be included on the food label. However, if a product contains an ingredient made from wheat but the ingredient does not contain protein, *wheat* does not have to be declared on the food label.

Sources: Code of Federal Regulations (CFR), www.gpoaccess.gov/cfr/retrieve.html; and Compliance Policy Guide (CPG), www.fda.gov/ora/orasrch.htm.

Appendix C
Gluten-Free Food Products

Enriched Gluten-Free Foods

The following are manufacturers of specially formulated enriched gluten-free foods

Ener-G Foods
Seattle, WA
Phone: 800-331-5222
Website: ener-g.com
Products: A variety of breads, buns/rolls/muffins, pizza crust, and other cereal foods are enriched with thiamin, riboflavin, niacin, folic acid, and iron.
Breads: Seattle brown loaf, corn loaf, new light brown rice loaf, light white rice loaf, light tapioca loaf, raisin loaf with eggs, brown rice loaf, egg-free raisin loaf, Papas loaf, rice starch loaf, white rice loaf, four flour loaf, tapioca loaf, white rice flax loaf
Buns/Rolls/Muffins: Tapioca hamburger buns, Seattle brown hamburger buns, brown rice hamburger buns, tapioca dinner rolls, white rice hamburger buns, tapioca hot dog buns, brown rice English muffins

Pizza Crust: Rice pizza shells

Other: Pound cake, brownies, doughnut holes, plain doughnuts, plain croutons, bread crumbs, broken melba toast

Enjoy Life Foods
3810 River Rd.
Schiller Park, IL 60176
Phone: 888-503-6560
Website: enjoylifefoods.com
Products: A variety of bagels, granola cereals, and snack bars are enriched with the B vitamins thiamin, riboflavin, niacin, folate, B_6 and C, as well as the minerals magnesium, iron, and calcium.
Bagels: Classic original and cinnamon raisin varieties
Granola Cereals: Cinnamon Crunch, Very Berry Crunch, and Cranapple Crunch
Snack Bars: Caramel Apple, Cocoa Loco, and Very Berry

Glutino
Laval, QC, Canada
Phone: 800-363-3438
Website: glutino.com
Products: A variety of breads, bagels, and other cereal foods are enriched with thiamin, riboflavin, niacin, vitamin B_6, iron, and calcium.
Breads: Premium bread with flaxseed, Premium bread with fiber, Premium corn bread, Premium cinnamon raisin bread
Bagels: Premium sesame bagel, Premium cinnamon raisin bagel, Premium plain bagel, Premium poppy seed bagel
Pizza Crust: Premium pizza crusts

Heartland's Finest

24291 Veterans Memorial Hwy.
Hilman, MI 49746
Phone: 888-658-8909
Website: heartlandsfinest.com
Products: One of its flours is enriched with thiamin, riboflavin, niacin, folic acid, and iron.
Flour: New Performance Blend flour

Kinnikinnick Foods, Inc.

10940-120 Street
Edmonton, AB, Canada T5H 3P7
Phone: 877-503-4466
Website: kinnikinnick.com
Products: A variety of breads, buns/muffins, bagels, and pizza crusts are enriched with thiamin, riboflavin, niacin, folic acid, and iron.
Breads: White sandwich bread, brown sandwich bread, cheese tapioca bread, Italian white tapioca bread, Many Wonder multigrain rice bread, raisin tapioca rice bread, Robins honey brown rice bread, tapioca rice bread, True Fiber multigrain rice bread, yeast-free tapioca bread
Buns/Muffins: Tapioca rice English muffins, tapioca rice hamburger buns, tapioca rice hot dog buns, tapioca rice multigrain seed and fiber buns, tapioca rice tray buns
Bagels: Tapioca rice cinnamon raisin bagels, tapioca rice New York style plain bagels, tapioca rice sesame bagels
Mixes: Tapioca rice bread mix
Pizza Crust: Ready-made crusts only

Maple Grove Food and Beverage
8175 Winston Churchill Blvd.
Norval, ON, Canada L0P 1K0
Phone: 905-451-7423
Website: maplegrovefoods.com
Products: A variety of pasta products are enriched with B
vitamins and iron.
Pasta: Pastariso brown rice fortified spaghetti, Pastato
potato gluten-free elbows, Pastato potato gluten-free
spaghetti

Perky's Natural Foods
3810 River Rd.
Schiller Park, IL 60176
Phone: 888-473-7597
Website: perkysnaturalfoods.com
Products: A variety of ready-to-eat breakfast cereals are
enriched with thiamin, riboflavin, niacin, folate, iron,
vitamin B_6, magnesium, and calcium.
Breakfast Cereals: Perky O's original, frosted, and apple
cinnamon

Manufacturers of Other Enriched Gluten-Free Foods

Genisoy
100 W. 5th Street, suite 700
Tulsa, OK 74103
Phone: 888-606-3829
Website: genisoy.com
Genisoy Soy Protein Bars: When this book went to press,
Chunky Peanut Butter Fudge and Creamy Peanut Yogurt
did not contain any gluten-containing ingredients.
(Genisoy's other soy protein bars are not gluten free.)

Always check labels to be sure product formulations have not changed. These bars are fortified with several vitamins and minerals, including calcium, thiamin, riboflavin, niacin, folic acid, and iron.

Genisoy Protein Crunch Bars: When this book went to press, Chocolate, Raspberry, Peanut Butter, and Chocolate Chip did not contain any gluten-containing ingredients. Always check labels to be sure product formulations have not changed. These bars are fortified with several vitamins and minerals, including calcium, thiamin, riboflavin, niacin, folic acid, and iron.

Gluten-Free Whole Grains

Amaranth

The following companies manufacture amaranth products:
Arrowhead Mills (arrowheadmills.com, 800-434-4246)
Bob's Red Mill (bobsredmill.com, 800-349-2173)
Nu-World Amaranth (nuworldamaranth.com, 630-369-6819)

Brown Rice

The following companies manufacture brown-rice products:
Arrowhead Mills (arrowheadmills.com, 800-434-4246)
Authentic Foods (authenticfoods.com, 800-806-4737)
Bob's Red Mill (bobsredmill.com, 800-349-2173)
Gifts of Nature (giftsofnature.net, 888-275-0003)

Buckwheat

The following companies manufacture buckwheat products:
Arrowhead Mills (arrowheadmills.com, 800-434-4246)
The Birkett Mills (thebirkettmills.com)
Bob's Red Mill (bobsredmill.com, 800-349-2173)

Millet

The following companies manufacture millet products:
Arrowhead Mills (arrowheadmills.com, 800-434-4246)
Bob's Red Mill (bobsredmill.com, 800-349-2173)

Oats

The following companies manufacture gluten-free oats:
Bob's Red Mill (bobsredmill.com, 800-349-2173)
Cream Hill Estates (pureoats.com, 866-727-3628)
Gifts of Nature (giftsofnature.net, 888-275-0003)
Gluten Free Oats (glutenfreeoats.com, 307-754-2058)
Only Oats (onlyoats.com, 866-461-3663)

Quinoa

The following companies manufacture quinoa products:
Arrowhead Mills (arrowheadmills.com, 800-434-4246)
Bob's Red Mill (bobsredmill.com, 800-349-2173)
Northern Quinoa Corporation (quinoa.com, 866-368-9304)
Quinoa Corporation (quinoa.net, 310-217-8125)

Sorghum

The following companies manufacture sorghum products:
Authentic Foods (authenticfoods.com, 800-806-4737)
Bob's Red Mill (bobsredmill.com, 800-349-2173)
Reiner's Farms—products sold through Manna Harvest
   (mannaharvest.net, 866-436-1390)
Shiloh Farms (shilohfarms.net)—products sold at the
   Gluten-Free Mall (glutenfreemall.com)
Twin Valley Mills (twinvalleymills.com, 402-279-3965)

Teff

The following companies manufacture teff products:
Bob's Red Mill (bobsredmill.com, 800-349-2173)
The Teff Company (teffco.com)

Whole Cornmeal (blue and yellow)

The following company manufactures whole-grain
cornmeal products:
Arrowhead Mills (arrowheadmills.com, 800-434-4246)

Wild Rice

The following companies manufacture wild-rice products:
Gibbs Wild Rice (gibbswildrice.com, 800-344-6378)

Gluten-Free Whole-Grain Cereals, Breads, Pastas, and Mixes

Most of the products listed here are made from 100 percent whole
grains. Some contain a mixture of grains, but the first ingredient

is a whole grain. For more information on these products, visit
the manufacturer's website.

Breakfast Cereals (Cold)

Amaranth Cereal Snaps (Nu-World Amaranth, nuworld
   amaranth.com)

Amaranth Cereal Snaps Cinnamon (Nu-world Amaranth,
   nuworldamaranth.com)

Amaranth Cereal Snaps Cocoa (Nu-World Amaranth, nuworld
   amaranth.com)

Amaranth Os (Nu-World Amaranth, nuworldamaranth.com)

Amaranth Os Peach (Nu-World Amaranth, nuworldamaranth.
   com)

Barbara's Brown Rice Crisps (Barbara's Bakery, barbarasbakery
   .com)

Barbara's Honey Rice Puffins (Barbara's Bakery, barbarasbakery
   .com)

Enjoy Life Foods Cinnamon Crunch granola (Enjoy Life Foods,
   enjoylifefoods.com)

Enjoy Life Foods Cranapple Crunch granola, (Enjoy Life Foods,
   enjoylifefoods.com)

Enjoy Life Foods Very Berry Crunch granola (Enjoy Life Foods,
   enjoylifefoods.com)

Envirokidz Koala Crisp (Nature's Path Foods, naturespath.com)

Erewhon Crispy Brown Rice (U.S. Mills, usmillsinc.com)

Erewhon Crispy Brown Rice with Mixed Berries (U.S. Mills,
   usmillsinc.com)

Erewhon Rice Twice (U.S. Mills, usmillsinc.com)

Nature's Path Crispy Rice (Nature's Path Foods, naturespath
   .com)

Puffed Amaranth Cereal (Nu-World Amaranth, nuworld
   amaranth.com)

Breakfast Cereals (Hot)

Amaranth Berry Delicious Hot Cereal (Nu-World Amaranth,
nuworldamaranth.com)

Creamy Brown Rice Farina (Bob's Red Mill, bobsredmill.com)

Erewhon Brown Rice Cream (U.S. Mills, usmillsinc.com)

Gluten-Free Mighty Tasty Hot Cereal (Bob's Red Mill,
bobsredmill.com)

Goji Berry with Blueberries (Only Oats, onlyoats.com)

Kiwi-Banana with Coconut (Only Oats, onlyoats.com)

Lundberg Hot 'n Creamy Rice Cereal (Lundberg Family Farms,
lundberg.com)

Organic Creamy Buckwheat Cereal (Bob's Red Mill,
bobsredmill.com)

Pocono Cream of Buckwheat (The Birkett Mills,
thebirkettmills.com)

Bread Products

Flatbread, amaranth-buckwheat (Nu-World Amaranth,
nuworldamaranth.com)

Flatbread, amaranth-garbanzo (Nu-World Amaranth,
nuworldamaranth.com)

Flatbread, amaranth-sorghum (Nu-World Amaranth,
nuworldamaranth.com)

Van's Gourmet Waffles (Van's International Foods, vansintl
.com)

Pasta

Ancient Harvest quinoa pasta—elbows, garden pagoda, spaghetti, rotelli, and shells, made from a blend of corn and
quinoa flour (Quinoa Corporation, quinoa.net)

Eden Foods buckwheat pasta (Eden Foods, edenfoods.com)

Lundberg brown-rice pasta—spaghetti, rotini, penne (Lundberg
Family Farms, lundberg.com)

Tinkyada brown-rice pasta—spaghetti, fusilli, spirals, penne, fettucini, shells, elbows, lasagna (Food Directions, tinkyada .com)

Mixes

Arrowhead Mills All Purpose Baking Mix (Arrowhead Mills, arrowheadmills.com)

Authentic Foods Pancake and Baking Mix (Authentic Foods, authenticfoods.com)

Bob's Red Mill Gluten-Free Hearty Whole Grain Bread Mix (Bob's Red Mill, bobsredmill.com)

Gluten-Free Pantry Brown Rice Baking Mix (Gluten-Free Pantry, glutenfree.com)

Gluten-Free Pantry Multi Grain Bread with Seeds Mix (Gluten-Free Pantry, glutenfree.com)

Gluten-Free Pantry Whole Grain Bread Mix (Gluten-Free Pantry, glutenfree.com)

Only Oats Muffin Mix (Only Oats, onlyoats.com)

Only Oats Pancake Mix (Only Oats, onlyoats.com)

Pamela's Amazing Wheat-Free Bread Mix (Pamela's Products, pamelasproducts.com)

Pamela's Ultimate Baking and Pancake Mix (Pamela's Products, pamelasproducts.com)

Sylvan Border Farm Classic Dark Bread Mix (Sylvan Border Farm, sylvanborderfarm.com)

Gluten-Free Products Made with Beans

Breakfast Cereal

Heartland's Finest CerOs, made with pinto bean flour— original, cinnamon, raspberry (Heartland's Finest, heartlandsfinest.com)

Flour

Arrowhead Mills—soy flour (Arrowhead Mills, arrowheadmills
.com)

Authentic Foods—Garfava flour, garbanzo bean flour (Authenic
Foods, authenticfoods.com)

Bob's Red Mill—black-bean flour, fava bean flour, garbanzo
bean flour, garbanzo and fava bean flour (Bob's Red Mill,
bobsredmill.com)

Heartland's Finest—whole navy bean flour, whole pinto bean
flour (Heartland's Finest, heartlandsfinest.com)

Pasta

Adrienne's Papadini Lentil Bean Pasta—penne, rotini, orzo,
linguini, spaghetti, conchigliette (Adrienne's, adriennes
gourmetfoods.com)

Heartland's Finest Navy Bean Flour Pasta—elbow macaroni,
spaghetti, linguini, rotini, ziti (Heartland's Finest,
heartlandsfinest.com)

Nutritional Content of Gluten-Free Flours and Grains

Manufacturers' Data

Amount	Cal	Chol	Pro	Fat	Fiber	Iron	Calcium	Thiamin	Riboflavin	Niacin	Folate
Amaranth bran flour (Nu–World Amaranth) ¼ cup											
32 g	103	18 g	5 g	1 g	3 g	20%	6%	n/a	n/a	n/a	n/a
Amaranth flour (Bob's Red Mill) ¼ cup											
30 g	110	20 g	4 g	2 g	3 g	n/a	n/a	n/a	n/a	n/a	n/a
Amaranth flour (Nu–World Amaranth) ¼ cup											
32 g	112	20 g	4 g	2 g	3 g	15%	4%	n/a	n/a	n/a	n/a
Amaranth grain (Arrowhead Mills) ¼ cup											
47 g	180	31 g	7 g	3 g	7 g	20%	8%	2%	6%	4%	n/a
Amaranth grain (Bob's Red Mill) ¼ cup											
49 g	180	32 g	7 g	3 g	7 g	n/a	n/a	n/a	n/a	n/a	n/a
Arrowroot starch (Bob's Red Mill) ¼ cup											
32 g	110	28 g	0 g	0 g	1 g	n/a	n/a	n/a	n/a	n/a	n/a
Black-bean flour (Bob's Red Mill) ¼ cup											
35 g	120	22 g	8 g	0 g	5 g	n/a	n/a	n/a	n/a	n/a	n/a

Amount	Cal	Chol	Pro	Fat	Fiber	Iron	Calcium	Thiamin	Riboflavin	Niacin	Folate
Brown-rice flour (Bob's Red Mill) ¼ cup											
40 g	140	31 g	3 g	1 g	1 g	n/a	n/a	n/a	n/a	n/a	n/a
Buckwheat flour (Arrowhead Mills) ⅓ cup											
30 g	115	20 g	5 g	1.5 g	6 g	6%	0%	2%	4%	6%	n/a
Buckwheat flour (Bob's Red Mill) ¼ cup											
30 g	100	21 g	4 g	1 g	4 g	n/a	n/a	n/a	n/a	n/a	n/a
Buckwheat groats (Arrowhead Mills) ¼ cup											
42 g	150	31 g	5 g	1 g	4 g	6%	0%	6%	6%	10%	n/a
Buckwheat groats (Bob's Red Mill) ¼ cup											
41 g	150	31 g	5 g	1 g	3 g	n/a	n/a	n/a	n/a	n/a	n/a
Buckwheat kernels (Bob's Red Mill) ¼ cup											
41 g	142	31 g	5 g	1 g	3 g	n/a	n/a	n/a	n/a	n/a	n/a
Cornmeal, blue (Arrowhead Mills) ⅓ cup											
35 g	130	25 g	3 g	1.5 g	5 g	4%	0%	6%	2%	2%	n/a
Cornmeal, yellow (Arrowhead Mills) ⅓ cup											
35 g	120	27 g	3 g	1 g	3 g	6%	0%	8%	2%	4%	n/a
Cornstarch (Bob's Red Mill) 1 tablespoon											
8 g	30	7 g	0 g	0 g	0 g	n/a	n/a	n/a	n/a	n/a	n/a

continued

Manufacturers' Data (continued)

Amount	Cal	Chol	Pro	Fat	Fiber	Iron	Calcium	Thiamin	Riboflavin	Niacin	Folate
Fava bean flour (Bob's Red Mill) ¼ cup											
33 g	110	19 g	9 g	0.5 g	8 g	n/a	n/a	n/a	n/a	n/a	n/a
Garbanzo bean flour (Bob's Red Mill) ¼ cup											
30 g	110	18 g	6 g	2 g	5 g	n/a	n/a	n/a	n/a	n/a	n/a
Navy bean flour (Heartland's Finest) ¼ cup											
36 g	130	23 g	7 g	0.5 g	6 g	15%	0%	n/a	n/a	n/a	n/a
Pinto bean flour (Heartland's Finest) ¼ cup											
36 g	140	24 g	8 g	1 g	5 g	15%	0%	n/a	n/a	n/a	n/a
Garbanzo and fava bean flour (Bob's Red Mill) ¼ cup											
30 g	110	18 g	6 g	1.5 g	6 g	n/a	n/a	n/a	n/a	n/a	n/a
Millet flour (Arrowhead Mills) ⅓ cup											
35 g	130	26 g	4 g	1.5 g	3 g	15%	0%	15%	8%	4%	n/a
Millet flour (Bob's Red Mill) ¼ cup											
30 g	110	22 g	3 g	1 g	4 g	n/a	n/a	n/a	n/a	n/a	n/a
Millet, hulled (Arrowhead Mills) ¼ cup											
44 g	150	33 g	4 g	1.5 g	1 g	15%	2%	15%	4%	4%	n/a
Millet, hulled (Bob's Red Mill) ⅛ cup											
25 g	90	18 g	3 g	1 g	4 g	n/a	n/a	n/a	n/a	n/a	n/a

Amount	Cal	Chol	Pro	Fat	Fiber	Iron	Calcium	Thiamin	Riboflavin	Niacin	Folate
Millet meal (Bob's Red Mill) ¼ cup											
47 g	150	34 g	5 g	1.5 g	3 g	n/a	n/a	n/a	n/a	n/a	n/a
Montina Pure Indian rice grass (Amazing Grains) ⅔ cup											
100 g	380	70 g	17 g	3 g	24 g	40%	8%	n/a	n/a	n/a	n/a
Potato flour (Bob's Red Mill) 3 tablespoons											
34 g	120	27 g	3 g	0.5 g	2 g	n/a	n/a	n/a	n/a	n/a	n/a
Potato starch (Bob's Red Mill) 1 tablespoon											
12 g	40	10 g	0 g	0 g	0 g	n/a	n/a	n/a	n/a	n/a	n/a
Quinoa flour (Bob's Red Mill) ¼ cup											
28 g	120	21 g	4 g	2 g	4 g	n/a	n/a	n/a	n/a	n/a	n/a
Quinoa grain (Arrowhead Mills) ⅓ cup											
43 g	160	30 g	6 g	2.5 g	3 g	20%	2%	6%	10%	6%	n/a
Quinoa grain (Bob's Red Mill) ¼ cup											
42 g	160	28 g	6 g	2.5 g	6.5 g	n/a	n/a	n/a	n/a	n/a	n/a
Sorghum flour (Bob's Red Mill) ¼ cup											
34 g	120	25 g	4 g	1 g	3 g	n/a	n/a	n/a	n/a	n/a	n/a
Sorghum flour (Twin Valley Mills) ¼ cup											
100 g	339	73 g	11.3 g	3.3 g	1.7 g	4.4 mg	n/a	n/a	n/a	n/a	n/a

continued

Manufacturers' Data (continued)

	Amount	Cal	Chol	Pro	Fat	Fiber	Iron	Calcium	Thiamin	Riboflavin	Niacin	Folate
Soy flour (Arrowhead Mills) ¼ cup	23 g	100	9 g	7 g	4.5 g	4 g	10%	4%	10%	15%	8%	n/a
Sweet rice flour (Bob's Red Mill) ¼ cup	51 g	180	40 g	3 g	0.5 g	1 g	n/a	n/a	n/a	n/a	n/a	n/a
Tapioca flour (Bob's Red Mill) ¼ cup	30 g	100	26 g	0 g	0 g	0 g	n/a	n/a	n/a	n/a	n/a	n/a
Teff (The Teff Company) ¼ cup	45 g	160	32 g	5 g	1 g	6 g	20%	8%	10%	2%	4%	n/a
Teff flour (Bob's Red Mill) ¼ cup	30 g	113	22 g	4 g	1 g	4 g	n/a	n/a	n/a	n/a	n/a	n/a
Teff grain (Bob's Red Mill) ¼ cup	45 g	160	33 g	6 g	1 g	6 g	n/a	n/a	n/a	n/a	n/a	n/a
White-rice flour (Bob's Red Mill) ¼ cup	40 g	150	32 g	2 g	0.5 g	1 g	n/a	n/a	n/a	n/a	n/a	n/a

Sources: Amazing Grains website, amazinggrains.com; Arrowhead Mills website, arrowheadmills.com; Bob's Red Mill website, bobs redmill.com; Heartland's Finest website, heartlandsfinest.com; Nu-World Amaranth website, nuworldamaranth.com; Teff Company website, teffco.com; and Twin Valley Mills website, twinvalleymills.com.

USDA Data

Amount	Cal	Chol	Pro	Fat	Fiber	Iron	Calcium	Thiamin	Riboflavin	Niacin	Folate
Amaranth ¼ cup											
49 g	182	32 g	7 g	3 g	4.5 g	3.7 mg	75 mg	0.04 mg	0.10 mg	0.63 mg	24 DFE
Arrowroot flour ¼ cup											
32 g	114	28 g	0 g	0 g	1 g	0.11 mg	13 mg	0 mg	0 mg	0 mg	2 DFE
Brown-rice flour ¼ cup											
40 g	143	30 g	3 g	1 g	2 g	0.78 mg	4 mg	0.18 mg	0.03 mg	2.5 mg	6 DFE
Buckwheat flour ¼ cup											
30 g	100	21 g	4 g	1 g	3 g	1.22 mg	12 mg	0.13 mg	0.06 mg	1.85 mg	16 DFE
Buckwheat groats ¼ cup											
41 g	142	31 g	5 g	1 g	4 g	1.01 mg	7 mg	0.09 mg	0.11 mg	2.11 mg	17 DFE
Corn flour, degermed, unenriched, yellow ¼ cup											
32 g	118	26 g	2 g	0.5 g	1 g	0.29 mg	1 mg	0.02 mg	0.02 mg	0.84 mg	15 DFE
Corn flour, masa, enriched, yellow ¼ cup											
29 g	104	22 g	3 g	1 g	n/a	2.05 mg	40 mg	0.41 mg	0.22 mg	2.81 mg	108 DFE
Corn flour, whole-grain, yellow ¼ cup											
29 g	106	22 g	2 g	1 g	2 g	0.7 mg	2 mg	0.07 mg	0.02 mg	0.56 mg	7 DFE

continued

USDA Data (continued)

Amount	Cal	Chol	Pro	Fat	Fiber	Iron	Calcium	Thiamin	Riboflavin	Niacin	Folate
Cornstarch ¼ cup											
32 g	122	29 g	0 g	0 g	0 g	0.15 mg	1 mg	0 mg	0 mg	0 mg	n/a
Garbanzo flour (chick-pea flour) ¼ cup											
23 g	89	13 g	5 g	2 g	2.5 g	1.12 mg	10 mg	0.11 mg	0.02 mg	0.41mg	101 DFE
Millet ¼ cup											
50 g	189	36 g	6 g	2 g	4 g	1.5 mg	4 mg	0.21 mg	0.15 mg	2.36 mg	42 DFE
Quinoa ¼ cup											
42.5 g	159	29 g	6 g	2 g	2.5 g	3.93 mg	26 mg	0.08 mg	0.17 mg	1.25 mg	21 DFE
Sorghum ¼ cup											
48 g	163	36 g	5 g	2 g	3 g	2.11 mg	13 mg	0.11 mg	0.07 mg	1.41 mg	n/a
White-rice flour ¼ cup											
39.5 g	145	32 g	2 g	1 g	1 g	0.14 mg	4 mg	0.06 mg	0.01 mg	1.02 mg	2 DFE

Source: U.S. Department of Agriculture, National Nutrient Database for Standard Reference, Release 19, 2006, available at nal.usda .gov/fnic/foodcomp/search/.

References

Alaedini A, Green PHR. Narrative review: Celiac disease: Understanding a complex autoimmune disorder. *Annals of Internal Medicine* 142 (2005): 289–98, available at www.annals.org/cgi/reprint/142/4/289 .pdf.

American Dietetic Association. Dietary fiber: An important link in the fight against heart disease. Nutrition Fact Sheet, www.eatright.org.

American Heart Association (AHA). Homocysteine, folic acid and cardiovascular disease. AHA website, www.americanheart.org/pre senter.jhtml?identifier=4677.

American Heart Association Scientific Statement: Diet and Lifestyle Recommendations Revision 2006. A Scientific Statement from the AHA Nutrition Committee. Available online at http://circ.aha journals.org/cgi/reprint/CIRCULATIONAHA.106.176158.

Arentz-Hansen H, Fleckenstein B, Molberg O, Scott H, Koning F, Jung G, Roepstorff P, Lundin KEA, Sollid LM. The molecular basis for oat intolerance in patients with celiac disease. *PLoS Medicine* 1(1) (2004): e1.

Baker PG, Read AE. Oats and barley toxicity in coeliac patients. *Postgraduate Medical Journal* 52 (1976): 264–68.

Barrionuevo A. Globalization in every loaf. *New York Times*, June 18, 2007, www.nytimes.com.

Benedictine Sisters of Perpetual Adoration. benedictinesisters.org.

Bickle K, Roark TR, Hsu S. Autoimmune bullous dermatoses: A review. *American Family Physician* 65 (2002): 1861–70.

Board on Science and Technology for International Development, National Research Council. *Lost Crops of Africa*. Vol. 1, *Grains*. Washington, DC: National Academy Press, 1996.

Bureau of Alcohol, Tobacco, Firearms, and Explosives website, www .atf.treas.gov/cgi-bin/atfgovsearch.cgi.

Campbell JA. Diet therapy of celiac disease and dermatitis herpetiformis. *World Review of Nutrition and Dietetics* 51 (1987): 189–233.

Catassi C, Rossini M, Ratsch I-M, Bearzi I, Santinelli A, Castagnani R, Pisani E, Coppa GV, Giorgi PI. Dose dependent effects of protracted ingestion of small amounts of gliadin in coeliac disease children: A clinical and jejunal morphometric study. *Gut* 34 (1993): 1515–19.

Celiac Sprue Association. CSA Recognition Seal Program. CSA website, www.csaceliacs.org/CSASealofRecognition.php.

Centers for Disease Control and Prevention. Folic acid: Frequently asked questions. CDC website, www.cdc.gov/ncbddd/folicacid/doc uments/FA_faqs_07_2005.pdf.

——— . Iron overload and hemochromatosis. CDC website, www .cdc.gov/hemochromatosis.

Chartrand LJ, Russo PA, Duhaime AG, Seidman EG. Wheat starch intolerance in patients with celiac disease. *Journal of the American Dietetic Association* 97 (1997): 612–18.

Code of Federal Regulations, www.gpoaccess.gov/cfr/retrieve.html.

Codex Alimentarius website, www.codexalimentarius.net/web/index _en.jsp.

Collin P, Thorell L, Kaukinen K, Maki M. The safe threshold for gluten contamination in gluten-free products. Can trace amounts be accepted in the treatment of coeliac disease? *Alimentary Pharmacology and Therapeutics* 19 (2004): 1277–83.

Cotton PA, Subar AF, Friday JE, Cook A. Dietary sources of nutrients among U.S. adults, 1994 to 1996. *Journal of the American Dietetic Association* 104 (2004): 921–30.

Dewar DH, Amato M, Pollock EL, Gonzalez-Cinca N, Wieser H, Ciclitira PJ. The toxicity of high molecular weight glutenin subunits of wheat to patients with coeliac disease. *European Journal of Gastro-enterology and Hepatology* 18 (2006): 483–91.

Dicke WK, Weijers HA, van de Kamer JH. Coeliac disease, II. The presence in wheat of a factor having a deleterious effect in cases of coeliac disease. *Acta Paediatrica* 42 (1953): 34–42.

Dissanayake AS, Truelove SC, Whitehead R. Lack of harmful effects of oats on the small intestinal mucosa in coeliac disease. *British Medical Journal* 4 (1974): 189–91.

Ener-G Foods. *Catalog of Gluten, Wheat and Dairy Free Products.* Ener-G Foods website, www.ener-g.com/pdf/Gffreewheatfreeallergyform.pdf.

The commission of European Communities. Commission Directive 2005/26/EC of 21 March 2005 establishing a list of food ingredients or substances provisionally excluded from Annex IIIa of Directive 2000/13/EC of the European Parliament and of the Council. Official Journal of the European Union. Available at Eur-Lex, http://eur-lex.europa.eu.

——— . Permanent exemption obtained for "allergen labeling" of wheat-based maltodextrin, glucose syrups, dextrose. Available at http://www.aaf-eu.org/PDF/Statement_on_permanent_exemption_obtained_for_allergen_labelling_11-2007.pdf.

European Food Safety Authority. Opinion of the Scientific Panel on Dietetic Products, Nutrition and Allergies on a request from the Commission related to a notification from AAC on wheat-based glucose syrups including dextrose pursuant to Article 6 paragraph 11 of Directive 2000/13/EC. *EFSA Journal* 126 (2004): 1–6, available at www.efsa.eu.int/science/nda/nda_opinions/catindex_en.html.

——— . Opinion of the Scientific Panel on Dietetic Products, Nutrition and Allergies on a request from the Commission related to a notification from AAC on wheat-based maltodextrins pursuant to Article 6 paragraph 11 of Directive 2000/13/EC. *EFSA Journal* 126 (2004): 1–6, available at www.efsa.eu.int/science/nda/nda_opinions/catindex_en.html.

————. Opinion of the Scientific Panel on Dietetic Products, Nutrition and Allergies on a request from the Commission related to a notification from Finnsugar on glucose syrups produced from barley starch pursuant to Article 6 paragraph 11 of Directive 2000/13/EC. *EFSA Journal* 126 (2004): 1–6, available at www.efsa.eu.int/science/nda/nda_opinions/catindex_en.html.

Fasano A, Berti I, Geraduzzi T, Not T, Colletti RB, Drago S, Elitsur Y, Green PH, Guandalini S, Hill ID, Pietzak M, Ventura A, Thorpe M, Kryszak D, Fornaroli F, Wasserman SS, Murray JA, Horvath K. Prevalence of celiac disease in at-risk and not-at-risk groups in the United States: A large multicenter study. *Archives of Internal Medicine* 163 (2003): 286–92.

Food and Drug Administration. Code of Federal Regulations. Available at www.fda.gov.

————. Food Labeling: Gluten-Free Labeling of Foods. Proposed Rule. 21 CFR Part 101, Docket No. 2005N-0279. *Federal Register* 72(14) (January 23, 2007), available at www.cfsan.fda.gov/~lrd/fr070123.html.

————. Food Standards: Amendment of Standards of Identity for Enriched Grain Products to Require Addition of Folic Acid (21 CFR Parts 136, 137, and 139). FDA/CFSAN *Federal Register* 61 FR 8781 (March 5, 1996), available at www.cfsan.fda.gov/~lrd/fr96305b.html.

————. Health claims: Soluble fiber from certain foods and risk of coronary heart disease. Code of Federal Regulations, 21 CFR 101.81. Available at www.fda.gov.

Food and Drug Administration, Center for Food Safety and Applied Nutrition. Advice to consumers: Food Allergen Labeling and Consumer Protection Act of 2004 Questions and Answers. FDA website, December 12, 2005, www.cfsan.fda.gov/~dms/alrgqa.html, accessed January 3, 2006.

————. Food Allergen Labeling and Consumer Protection Act of 2004 (Title II of Public Law 108-282). FDA website, August 12, 2004, www.cfsan.fda.gov/~dms/alrgact.html, accessed January 3, 2006.

———— . *Food Allergen Labeling and Consumer Protection Act of 2004 (Title II of Public Law 108-282).* Report to the U.S. Senate and the U.S. House of Representatives, July 2006 (discussion of cross-contact). FDA website, www.cfsan.fda.gov/~acrobat/alrgrep .pdf.

———— . Guidance for industry: Questions and answers regarding food allergens, including the Food Allergen Labeling and Consumer Protection Act of 2004 (Edition 2); Final guidance. FDA website, www.cfsan.fda.gov/~dms/alrguid2.html, December 14, 2005, accessed January 3, 2006.

———— . Trans fat now listed with saturated fat and cholesterol on the Nutrition Facts label. FDA website, www.cfsan.fda.gov/~dms/trans fat.html, last updated January 1, 2006.

Food and Nutrition Board, Institute of Medicine. Dietary reference intakes: Elements. *DRI Summary Tables,* Institute of Medicine website, www.iom.edu/Object.File/Master/7/294/0.pdf.

———— . *Dietary Reference Intakes for Calcium, Phosphorus, Magnesium, Vitamin D, and Fluoride.* Washington, DC: National Academies Press, 1997, available at www.nap.edu/books/0309063507/html/ index.html.

———— . *Dietary Reference Intakes for Energy, Carbohydrate, Fiber, Fat, Fatty Acids, Cholesterol, Protein, and Amino Acids.* Washington, DC: National Academies Press, 2002, available at http://books.nap .edu/books/0309085373/html/.

———— . *Dietary Reference Intakes for Thiamin, Riboflavin, Niacin, Vitamin B_6, Folate, Vitamin B_{12}, Pantothenic Acid, Biotin, and Choline.* Washington, DC: National Academies Press, 1998, available at www.nap.edu/books/0309065542/html/index.html.

———— . *Dietary Reference Intakes for Vitamin A, Vitamin K, Arsenic, Boron, Chromium, Copper, Iodine, Iron, Manganese, Molybdenum, Nickel, Silicon, Vanadium, and Zinc.* Washington, DC: National Academies Press, 2000, available at www.nap .edu/books/0309072794/html/.

————— . *Dietary Reference Intakes: Guiding Principles for Nutrition Labeling and Fortification.* Washington, DC: National Academies Press, 2003, available at http://nap.edu/books/0309091438/html/47.html.

————— . Dietary reference intakes: Macronutrients. *DRI Summary Tables*, Institute of Medicine website, www.iom.edu/Object.File/Master/7/300/0.pdf.

————— . Dietary reference intakes: Vitamins. *DRI Summary Tables*, Institute of Medicine website, www.iom.edu/Object.File/Master/7/296/0.pdf.

Gluten-Free Certification Organization website, www.gfco.org.

Gluten-Free Living (magazine), www.glutenfreeliving.com.

Haas SV. The value of the banana in the treatment of celiac disease. *American Journal of Diseases of Children* 28 (1924): 421–37.

Hardman CM, Garioch JJ, Leonard JN, Thomas HJW, Walker MM, Lortan JE, Lister A, Fry L. Absence of toxicity of oats in patients with dermatitis herpetiformis. *New England Journal of Medicine* 337 (1997): 1884–87.

Hernando A, Mujico JR, Juanas D, Mendez E. Confirmation of the cereal type in oat products highly contaminated with gluten. *Journal of the American Dietetic Association* 106 (2006): 665.

Hoffenberg EJ, Haas J, Drescher A, Barnhurst R, Osberg I, Bao F, Eisenbarth G. A trial of oats in children with newly diagnosed celiac disease. *Journal of Pediatrics* 137 (2000): 361–66.

Hogberg L, Laurin P, Faith-Magnusson K, Grant C, Grodzinsky E, Jansson G, Ascher H, Browaldh L, Hammersjo JA, Lindberg E, Myrdal U, Stenhammar L. Oats to children with newly diagnosed coeliac disease: A randomized double blind study. *Gut* 53 (2004): 649–54.

Holm K, Maki M, Vuolteenaho N, Mustalahti K, Ashorn M, Ruuska T. Oats in the treatment of childhood coeliac disease: A 2-year controlled trial and a long-term clinical follow-up study. *Alimentary Pharmacology and Therapeutics* 23 (2006): 1463–72.

Holt LE. Celiac disease—what is it? *Journal of Pediatrics* 46 (1955): 369–79.

Janatuinen EK, Kemppainen TA, Julkunen RJK, Kosma V-M, Mäki M, Heikkinen M, Uusitupa MIJ. No harm from five year ingestion of oats in coeliac disease. *Gut* 50 (2002): 332–35.

Janatuinen EK, Kemppainen TA, Pikkarainen PH, Holm KH, Kosma V-M, Uusitupa MIJ, Mäki M, Julkunen RJK. Lack of cellular and humoral immunological responses to oats in adults with coeliac disease. *Gut* 46 (2000): 327–31.

Janatuinen EK, Pikkarainen PH, Kemppainen TA, Kosma V-M, Järvinen MK, Uusitupa MIJ, Julkunen RJK. A comparison of diets with and without oats in adults with celiac disease. *New England Journal of Medicine* 333 (1995): 1033–37.

Joint FAO/WHO Food Standards Program. Report of the 29th session of the Codex Committee on Nutrition and Foods for Special Dietary Uses. ALINORM 08/31/26, November 2007, 50–51.

Joint FAO/WHO Food Standards Program, Codex Committee on Nutrition and Foods for Special Dietary Uses. Draft revised standard for gluten-free foods. CX/NFSDU 98/4. July 1998, 1–4.

Kasarda DD. Gluten and gliadin: Precipitation factors in coeliac disease. In *Coeliac Disease: Proceedings of the Seventh International Symposium on Coeliac Disease*, edited by M Maki, P Collin, and JC Visakorpi, 195–212. Tampere, Finland: Celiac Disease Study Group, 1997.

Lichtenstein AH, Appel LJ, Brands M, Carnethon M, et al. Diet and lifestyle recommendations revision 2006: A scientific statement from the American Heart Association Nutrition Committee, *Circulation* 114 (2006): 82–96, http://circ.ahajournals .org/cgi/reprint/CIRCULATIONAHA.106.176158.

Lundin KE, Nilsen EM, Scott HG, Loberg EM, Gjoen A, Bratlie J, Skar V, Mendez E, Lovik A, Kett K. Oats induced villous atrophy in coeliac disease. *Gut* 52 (2003): 1649–52.

Mariani P, et al. The gluten-free diet: A nutritional risk factor for adolescents with celiac disease? *Journal of Pediatric Gastroenterology and Nutrition* 27 (1998): 519–23.

McBean LD, Miller GD. Allaying fears and fallacies about lactose intolerance. *Journal of the American Dietetic Association* 98 (1998): 671–76.

Moulton ALC. The place of oats in the coeliac diet. *Archives of Disease in Childhood* 34 (1959): 51–55.

Murray JA. The widening spectrum of celiac disease. *American Journal of Clinical Nutrition* 69 (1999): 354–65, available at www.ajcn.org.

National Institute of Arthritis and Musculoskeletal and Skin Diseases (NIAMS). What people with celiac disease need to know about osteoporosis. National Institutes of Health, Department of Health and Human Services, NIAMS website, www.niams.nih.gov/bone/hi/bowel/celiac.htm.

National Institute of Diabetes and Digestive and Kidney Diseases (NIDDK). Celiac disease. NIH Publication No. 07-4269. National Digestive Diseases Information Clearinghouse, August 2007, NIDDK website, http://digestive.niddk.nih.gov/ddiseases/pubs/celiac/.

National Institutes of Health Consensus Development Program. Consensus Development Conference Statement. NIH Consensus Development Conference on Celiac Disease, June 28–30, 2004, http://consensus.nih.gov/2004/2004CeliacDisease118html.htm.

Oelke EA, et al. Wild rice. *Alternative Field Crops Manual.* University of Wisconsin, University of Minnesota, last updated December 2, 1997. NewCROP, Purdue University, www.hort.purdue.edu/newcrop/afcm/wildrice.html.

Office of Dietary Supplements (ODS), National Institutes of Health. Dietary supplement fact sheet: Folate. ODS website, www.ods.od.nih.gov/factsheets/folate.asp.

——— . Dietary supplement fact sheet: Iron. ODS website, http://ods.od.nih.gov/factsheets/iron.asp.

Office of the Surgeon General. *Bone Health and Osteoporosis: A Report of the Surgeon General.* Rockville, MD: U.S. Department

of Health and Human Services, 2004, www.surgeongeneral
.gov/library.

Peraaho M, Kaukinen K, Mustalahti K, Vuolteenaho N, Mäki M, Laippala P, Collin P. Effect of oats-containing gluten-free diet on symptoms and quality of life in coeliac disease: A randomized study. *Scandinavian Journal of Gastroenterology* 39 (2004): 27–31.

Position of the American Dietetic Association: Health implications of dietary fiber. *Journal of the American Dietetic Association* 102 (2002): 993–1000.

Reunala T, Collin P, Holm K, Pikkarainen P, Miettinen A, Vuolteen-aho N, Mäki M. Tolerance to oats in dermatitis herpetiformis. *Gut* 43 (1998): 490–93.

Sake-World website, www.sake-world.com.

Srinivasan U, Leonard N, Jones E, Kasarda DD, Weir DG, O'Farrelly C, Feighery C. Absence of oats toxicity in adult coeliac disease. *British Medical Journal* 313 (1996): 1300–1301.

Steward JS. History of the coeliac condition. Available online at http://osiris.sunderland.ac.uk/~csorel/hist.htm.

Storsrud S, Olsson M, Arvidsson Lenner R, Nilsson LA, Kilander A. Adult coeliac patients do tolerate large amounts of oats. *European Journal of Clinical Nutrition* 57 (2003): 163–69.

Tatham AS, et al. Characterisation of the major prolamins of tef and finger millet. *Journal of Cereal Science* 24 (1996): 65–71.

Thompson T. Folate, iron, and fiber contents of the gluten-free diet. *Journal of the American Dietetic Association* 100 (2000): 1389–96.

——— . Gluten contamination of commercial oat products in the United States. *New England Journal of Medicine* 351 (2004): 2021–22.

——— . Oats and the gluten-free diet. *Journal of the American Dietetic Association* 103 (2003): 376–79.

——— . Thiamin, riboflavin, and niacin contents of the gluten-free diet: Is there cause for concern? *Journal of the American Dietetic Association* 99 (1999): 858–62.

————. Wheat starch, gliadin, and the gluten-free diet. *Journal of the American Dietetic Association* 101 (2001): 1456.

Thompson T, Dennis M, Higgins LA, Lee AR, Sharrett MK. Gluten-free diet survey: Are Americans with coeliac disease consuming recommended amounts of fiber, iron, calcium and grain foods? *Journal of Human Nutrition and Dietetics* 18 (2005): 163–69.

U.S. Department of Agriculture. MyPyramid.gov, www.mypyramid .gov.

U.S. Department of Agriculture, Agricultural Research Service. National Nutrient Database for Standard Reference, Release 19 (2006), www.nal.usda.gov/fnic/foodcomp/search/.

U.S. Department of Agriculture, Food and Nutrition Information Center. Early Food Guides (1894–1940). *Historical Food Guides Background and Development*, last modified September 2002, www .nal.usda.gov/fnic/history/early.htm.

U.S. Department of Agriculture, Food Safety and Inspection Service (FSIS). Food safety: Natural flavorings on meat and poultry labels. *Help: Common Questions*, FSIS website, last modified February 14, 2006, www.fsis.usda.gov/Help/FAQs_Flavorings/ index.asp.

————. Questions and answers related to ingredients of public health concern. FSIS website, www.fsis.usda.gov/OPPDE/rdad/FSISNo tices/FAQs_for_Notice_45-05.pdf, accessed March 1, 2006.

————. Verification of activities related to an establishment's controls for the use of ingredients of public health concern. FSIS Notice 45-05. FSIS website, www.fsis.usda.gov/regulations_&_policies/ Notice_45-05/index.asp, accessed March 1, 2006.

U.S. Department of Health and Human Services. *Dietary Guidelines for Americans, 2005.* www.health.gov/dietaryguidelines/ dga2005/document/.

U.S. Department of Health and Human Services. Executive Summary of the Dietary Guidelines for Americans, 2005. www.health. gov/dietaryguidelines/dga2005/document/html/executivesummary .htm.

WHO Scientific Group on the Prevention and Management of Osteoporosis. *Prevention and Management of Osteoporosis.* WHO Techni-
cal Report Series No. 921. Geneva: World Health Organization,
2003, http://whqlibdoc.who.int/trs/WHO_TRS_921.pdf.

Wikipedia, http://en.wikipedia.org. Alcoholic beverage accessed
November 26, 2007. Distillation accessed November 26, 2007.
Brewing accessed November 26, 2007.

Zeman FJ. *Clinical Nutrition and Dietetics.* New York: Macmillan,
1991.

Index

About the Author

Tricia Thompson, M.S., RD, is a nutrition consultant, author, and speaker specializing in celiac disease and the gluten-free diet. She has written numerous articles for both scientific and popular readers, including those that have appeared in *Gluten-Free Living* magazine, the *Journal of the American Dietetic Association*, the *Journal of Human Nutrition and Dietetics*, and the *New England Journal of Medicine*.

Tricia is the author of the American Dietetic Association's booklet Celiac Disease Nutrition Guide, 2nd edition, and a contributing author to the American Dietetic Association's Nutrition Care Manual (celiac disease section). She is a working group member of the Association's Evidence Analysis Library project on gluten intolerance. She is also a member of the dietitian advisory board of *Gluten-Free Living* magazine and the author of the magazine's Neglected Nutrition series.

Tricia has a M.S. in nutrition from Tufts University in Boston, Massachusetts, and a B.A. in English Literature from Middlebury College in Vermont. She completed her dietetic internship at the Frances Stern Nutrition Center at the New England Medical Center in Boston.

For more information about the gluten-free diet, visit Tricia's website at glutenfreedietitian.com.